MW01204997

Toward a genuine spirituality

**Our minds are circumscribed
by our immediate reality, but
we stop short at the thought of it.**

by Matt Berry

Published by

Universal Publishers/uPUBLISH.com

USA 1999

http://www.upublish.com/books/berry.htm

ISBN: 1-58112-837-1

Table of Contents

My Slice of Eternity

In life we confuse equation with nature and settle into our recliners, buoyed with incredible smugness by our day-to-day routine. If, however, this routine were to be unceremoniously pulled out from under us, we would find ourselves prostrate upon the hard earth ... upon the rude truth: we would not know where or how to begin anew, since we had thought that the *principle* was our comfort. But what do we do? We kneel and work out new equations, tearing out pages from our scratch pad as quickly as we fill them with numbers and symbols ... while the natural phenomenon, habit, on its own, slowly weaves out a new fabric for us. One day the fabric holds, and once again we believe ourselves to float "above reality." We are content again. "The principle!"

But what if I discarded all principle from the outset? Set fire to all the scraps of paper around me? What if I found it possible to have wicked thoughts even within the sterilized corridor of science? What if I were no longer content with the mere observation of human behavior? What if instead I sought out forces ... immediate control? Just as the engineer seeks out force and builds an apparatus to apply that force, I would seek out natural influences ... to myself ... for myself ... with no other rule or law but this: to gain more and more personal force.

What if, to my horror, these forces were more basic ... more simplistic than I had wished them to be? I find myself an "automated process" where every occasion for human meaningfulness reduces itself all too quickly to a mechanical clarity. What if it were this horror — honesty — that choked me so that I could no longer speak of the human condition with any sense of dignity? What if I had the same face as always, but with a new apparatus to see that face, for the first time, and so as to be able finally to recognize myself? To suffer an identity crisis *because I have absolutely no doubt as to who and what I am.* And just só, what if I acquired a new apparatus to hear my own voice without the reverberations of that voice upon my own skull, and so that this time I recognize that foreign voice as my own?

With this horrible, rigorous science, I observe my thoughts in their daily routine, as I would a white rat in the labyrinth, working its way through incredible complexities, all toward a very simple end ... all of my aspirations and virtues sniffling toward this same piece of cheese. I keep my chin up, follow my nose back down that ancient path, turning my head left and right in search of that older, more savage means which had glory and dignity for an end ... but I stop even before this last virtue. It only smells of nobility.

I can no longer worship kings, or the Lord, or a universal being. I have no appetite for new ideas. I no longer want to get behind it all ... to seek out that all encompassing truth, for I already have it in my hands. The ultimate truth is a wedge of cheese. These days if I kneel at all, I kneel and tinker with the mechanical force of stimulus and response ... kneel before this white rat in its maze and press the cheese into the double-mirrored corridor of my choosing. The rat, once arrived — and to my horror, it always arrives — looks left and right to the thousand thousand iterations of itself ... each iteration pressing that cheese a little more precisely, pat into this selfsame corner ... each iteration inching toward the sublime perfection of itself.

I find no humor in this, so why does Fate go on and on with these ridiculous attempts? I lack a sense for humor, perhaps. Well, I can develop even that, if there were but cheese enough and time.

Here is another bad joke which I must endure: man as machine had hitherto been the horror of my life, but now it promises to become my newest hope ... and though I have grown wary of all hopes, I know of no deeper reality than this mechanical force, of no other means of getting to the other side of the equation of life than to pursue greater and greater natural force from the immediate world ... energy ... to build out of myself an apparatus not only for the application of force, but for the acquisition of *more* force.

8

This has become something like a religion with me. Of course, it is really only madness ... of course, I am mad ... but in my own defense, it is only self-control, in every applicable sense of the word, that constitutes my madness. The day I found myself institutionalized within a society which forbade my own control over myself, I resigned myself to this padded cell. I consider myself lucky. A few generations ago they would have burned me at the stake; now, my words are tolerated ... but never my force ... my tools for altering my own destiny and thereby the destiny of others ... for once I set tools to the hinges of this door I will be wrestled to the ground again, injected with the palliatives of the newest, most advanced morality, and hustled into a stronger cell.

But what do I care? I am in the pursuit of force, if not its possession. One day, perhaps, I may even harness it. And what would a little control do for me? The claim is modest enough: I would then have the block and tackle to lower this oversized rodent into a new labyrinth. I would scoff at the absurdity of my circumstance, make of my world a cornucopia of cheeses. It would smell of a newer hope ... of a last hope, and this new, final hope would become my only possible response. In the pursuit of what? A slice of eternity, a few priceless jewels of recollection to set in velvet, the gratitude of a few friends, a new path toward dignity ...

The Descent of a Realist

The profit-loss man, lacking all taste, has at least purchased a little tact through the demands of the marketplace: he has had to influence people on a daily basis and therefore knows how to move people to his own advantage. Those who have been sheltered by luxury and good taste have never felt themselves moved in this manner and thus confuse his salesmanship with taste; perhaps they even feel themselves indebted to him. It may be said that a refined and inherited taste preserves and cultivates only what tact will harvest later. That is to say, the tactful acquire the sensibilities of the privileged ... and soon thereafter, their graceful signatures. Tact over taste — it seems to conform to the natural justice of the species ... as when the powerful have lost their grip on the fundamentals to that power and so lose it over a truffle.

Introduction   :

3

Imagine the human task as a kind of game with clearly defined rules:

1. The only legitimate reality is that which we verify with our senses. Consequently, reality is nothing more than surface and the relationships between surfaces.

2. "Mind," "Depth," "Meaning," "Ideas," "Other Worlds," are *un*real ... errors ... figments of an error-making organ, the brain.

In short, wherever we can not reduce something "human" to mechanical explanation what we really have is fear.

The Mind adds Infinity, then is divided by Reality which must then take away Infinity again to equal the Human Condition. That is, we are less in mind for wanting to be more than reality ... that is, we are more or less fools.

Atheism

And cynicism shall set you free.

Patience is a virtue ... and God has kept me waiting for so long that I have finally had to admit this one gift from and evidence of *Him*. I still wait, and he still teaches this last lesson ... this teacher of teachers. Very soon now, my Patience will wax eternal.

No hero really wants to die for something as much as he wants to *live on in the minds of others*. The contentment of our sacrificial victims, then, requires our assistance: we must not only throw them into the volcano but must always bear them in mind.

However, the *ultimate sacrifice*, from a purely Christian viewpoint, would be to sacrifice oneself for all of humanity without any reward whatsoever — even the endurance of one's identity in the mind of others. It is thus that God will soon redeem all and make that final, pure sacrifice ... as only God can do. It pains me to think about it. All this while *we* have been waiting for *Him*, when it is *He* who has been waiting for *us*.

A fable: After several painful attempts, an ostrich concluded that it was unable to fly. *"Somehow I must account for these feathers"* it thought to itself. One day it spotted a gull floating on the sea. *"Water is a lot like air and will have to do. Perhaps this is what it would be like to fly!"* Struggling up through the beating surf, it grew weary and drowned.

Moral: I do not have to account for anything. If I inherit "mind" or "soul" or "quest for meaning" or "the right to act" ... or some other ostrich-feathered desire for something *"beyond,"* I do not have to make an accounting for it ... put it to any kind of use ... prove it or disprove it. Better to laugh at my feathers and hop around a bit ... even show them off maybe.

Why I should not have to be an atheist: This is not a God-AntiGod world.

Why I am an atheist: God is a cultural reality ... just as an eye patch is a reality.

Answering the Christian: *Why I have not abandoned myself to the Devil:* If God is a white eye patch, then the devil is a black one.

How much ground have we already conceded to the devil! If I read a thousand books on Christ and a single word of the devil's I am a Satanist. The devil's *appeal?* A single word from the devil on the Christian scale is so heavy as to make all of the books on goodness mere air ... one end of the scale crashes to the floor so violently that even the parishioners wake up ... and take notes ... as nothing spices up a sermon so much as a few wicked thoughts.

The Institution

13

Perhaps it is *weakness* that accounts for society's dramatic evolution: against the superior individual, two cowards had to come together to defend themselves.

Or is it *strength* that accounts for civilization? ... a single individual so strong that he conquered all others ... or perhaps the others simply cowered under his protection, just as a dog cowers under a tree during a storm. But then if this is so, if we see these "others" as essential to the definition of the city, have we not again suggested that our city is made up of weakness and cowardice? And if so, how can anyone, after coming across this discovery, expect to value existence through the standard of community spirit?

14

There is a type of human that must be contained, a type which will send the whole machine of civilization flying apart if allowed to accelerate beyond its capacity. It is one of the oldest cogs of civilization ... formerly called the "slave," but now called the "good citizen."

15

This man has a dull exterior, but when I brush up against him, in opposition or polite conversation, he gains a luster, which only begins to cloud over again when a third person enters the room.

16

Youth often suffer from an identity crisis because we insist that they be someone else ... that they abandon themselves to become a piece in our jigsaw puzzle. We twist them this way and that in the hope that they might fit into our perspective of ourselves. In short, they suffer *our* identity crisis ... and then we criticize them for it.

17

Every principle for personal growth, once institutionalized, shifts from serving as a vehicle for self-actualization to serving the actualization of the vehicle itself. We are no longer nurtured, but managed.

18

Duty and Meaning: Where our duty has no personal meaning we wish for a little understanding from our superiors. But they can spare none, for without our duty, their meaninglessness is exposed.

19

We have outlawed the influence of the church upon the state ... and now the state enforces a herd morality of its own upon us. Then what do we care of the separation of church and state? The separation from both church and state is rather the thing necessary.

20

The only irrefutable systems of philosophy are those we preserve with physical force.

Most of our thoughts on world peace descend from institutions with a vested interest in preserving the invisibility of their dominance. No one avoids conflict like an established conqueror. Under this light, Christian peace was indeed the end of war ... as the final step of its conquest.

To achieve peace *for all,* the disadvantaged must be given a false "advantage" that they can call their own: patriotism as "liberty" ... or remaining with one's own cultural inheritance as "freedom of worship," for example. We hold up every label which secures the tractability of the individual, such as "good citizenship" or "virtuous." The contentment of the masses depends upon this trade of an illusory advantage for an actual one — as does the illusory contentment of the powerful few.

Why I flee from all social movements: It is not their threat to tear all non-members apart as much as it is the morass I would have to wade through in search of an acceptable stand. Authenticity betrays a need for *cleanliness* that perhaps outweighs the destiny of all mankind ... but I'll stop here; I sully myself with the explanation.

As reformers, we resent not only our opponents but most of all the honest critics of our own devices and motives. Not one motive of ours can be tinkered with; not one ray of light enter our own closets. Our reformation of other people is not as much a will to improve mankind as it is a diversion away from our own failings and responsibilities.

A man should not build an institution until all his creative powers have been exhausted on something worthwhile.

What is our weakness? Not the falsehood of our inherited morality, nor its harm, but that we *need* it.

Civilized Behavior and the Last Banana

I am rude when I do not point my act toward the other person. I can break any rule of etiquette but this and keep the other's sympathy.

I appear to protect her, and that is more than a duty I impose upon myself. I do not know what would become of me if I did not *have* to protect my angel ... *but how she fully justifies her independence!* And I, being a rational man, must now confront the brutality of my "protecting her."

As an ideal we would be king and queen. "What? The last banana? Why, to hell with it, *you* have it, dear. We'll send George out for them one at a time." As a reality, it's a matter of how far up the ladder of evolution we find ourselves at that particular moment.

We suffer from all sorts of limitations, but the limits of civilized behavior are often the hardest to bear, and the closer the acquaintance the more difficult the burden. We know full well the unbending laws of nature but expect a friend to "give in" a little, and the longer we love the more we grow accustomed to this "giving in." Then one day he absolutely refuses to share a banana and we go ape.

Man is the reasonable ape which will swing from tree to tree to get the banana, but when satisfied, will sit and brood about how his logic should not have to swing about with such indignity ... should not have to leave one vine for another, for there is no real "connection" after all. What he really should do, he decides, is find one infinitely long vine on an infinitely tall tree by which he might have the whole jungle at his disposal, or the hell with it, he won't swing at all. This lasts for a few hours or so, depending upon the metabolism of the ape, but if he is a professional logician, then his metabolism is quite low, and so the hours of non-foraging can be quite extensive, but not so extensive that they cannot be calculated with precision: he broods, without fail, between the hours of nine to five ... then leaps to the nearest vine, confused by his unreasonable craving for bananas, but which he quickly and decisively refutes again by eating a few.

The Unselfish and their Charity

Unselfishness is not concerned with the other person. On the contrary, it has emptied itself and is only concerned with filling itself again ... *by emptying itself.* It arrives, not as a polite guest, but as an impossible demand, a starving guest who refuses all food with the excuse, "But I'm hungry ... do you have an emetic?"

33

Taking a step back, out of range, is healthier than turning the other cheek. It is also more benevolent.

34

How to kill what I love: do everything for the beloved ... mercy, pity, help in every way ... never let the beloved strain a muscle. Ah, but to be *truly* kind ... one would be crucified for that.

35

I am convinced that if we were to die and enter paradise the devil would ruin it all by having the damned reach their hands through the gates, begging for alms and forgiveness — and the greater the sincerity of the devil, the greater our misery.

36

He who has a heart of gold is pure in heart: Here is a rich man who has his strongbox full of coins, with no room for more. He casts what remains to the feet of the less fortunate, nonchalantly and perhaps with an ounce of arrogance ... but also with a pound of foolhardiness, for where else might he have put these trifles and without effecting such a return from their black hearts?

They must pay for the respect they now owe, all the more grudgingly when the debt is forgiven: a humble gratitude, from the poor to the rich, becomes another word for humiliation, and this is a debt which *must* be paid with the coin of resentment. It is impossible both to *owe* and to be pure in heart. ... a warning to those who owe tithes to anyone other than themselves.

The Impossible Individual

37

To vilify someone: first method, expose him as an outsider to our morality (an easy task, since "morality," as commonly understood, is artificial). Second method, expose him as just another member of the herd (even easier).

38

I cannot be an individual without social attachment. How else would I get the training? And from whom would I flee?

39

The "Truth" is not something which must be defended. If "Truth" is what is absolutely necessary to well-being, then it need only be pointed out. That which we have been defending at all costs is only what is necessary to the well-being of *our group.*

But the fact that we defend the needs of our group at the very expense of our own well-being, and successfully I might add, damages my argument. For certainly, if my own well-being were pointed out, wouldn't I attempt to secure it? Wrong question. Why don't I try? ... and how did I learn that I *should* try? From that smaller group, the individualists? It's easy to forget that individualism is a social movement. So, what am I seeking? For I need my group ...

40

How can I put this crowd behind me and shut them up ... *after* we have abandoned each other?

The subjective world is unshared and isolated, each of us contained in our own bubble of illusion and calling it the universe, each of us feeling this universe in common with all of humanity ... and all the more lonely for it.

42

Individualism is a disease of the social animal for which one amputates a large part of oneself in the hope of a cure.

43

To grow one must never expose one's roots to sunlight ... just as one must never hide one's foliage. To use a different metaphor, one must build a door between private and social contexts ... one which we lock shut.

44

We are spiraling; that is sure. But are we rising or falling? And if we are indeed rising ... as is the end of all our efforts and sufferings ... are we only rising within the stratum of our class?

The Public Animal

45

"Are you higher or lower in rank?" The first question one asks every stranger ... in spite of oneself.

46

A: You say that I am not easy to work with ... which tells me that I am not exploitable.

B: You say that I am easy to work with ... which tells me that you are easily taken.

47

In most philosophical arguments there emerges a leader whose arguments do not follow, thereby.

48

Grief and laughter purify, and both require suffering: respectively, ours or our neighbor's.

49

That which tears at the moral fabric of society is of the same claw of that which condemns the attack.

50

It is not difficult to find a man who accepts himself as a pin cushion, and if he is under our care, we protect him from himself and from the others who must find something to prick, if for no other reason than to prove that they *can* prick.

This noble act — drawing our own sharp weapons and keeping the others at bay — is not duty. On the contrary, it is one of the pleasures of the flesh, for we too must prove that we can prick.

51

The difference between men and women: Put a kitten into a room full of fourteen year old boys. Put another kitten into a room full of fourteen year old girls. Assure them that no one will oversee or condemn their actions. What is the lesson here? By the time we are mature enough to modify our roles of gender half of us already have one cat on our conscience while the other half condemn us with an equal viciousness yet unequal degree of effort

— unequal, because the tenderhearted find the inertia of justice and mercy forever at their backs.

* The difference between a group of fourteen year old boys and a solitary boy of the same age is just as striking — not only because the solitary boy lacks cruelty, but that when returned to the group, the subsequent reactions of *revenge, justice* and *mercy* are also lacking. He would not think of fleeing from the guilt, for that would be tantamount to fleeing from his group. No, he would rather suffer as an accomplice, which he can do vicariously by his refusal to pass judgment on the matter.

52

From the horrible monster, *Reality*, we organize ourselves behind a standard, in mass, ... in tactically brilliant retreats. Forever looking for a fixed, naturally fortified position from which to make a final stand. A few of us exhaust ourselves in the attempt, see the futility, stray, then unconditionally surrender all that we have. The irony is that only then do we find our sanctuary ... but within the walls of our former fear, *Realism*, and the new horror is not that we have become, nor even that we always have been, this solitary monster, but that now the others have found us out.

53

We were not born *realists*, nor did we make a choice. The civilized climb from *what-is* to the peak of *what-should-be* has been so mob-driven and the height so fearsome that we can not even contemplate the solitary descent back down to the truth. And it is no matter that this problem never shows itself to our consciousness — for we are not without help from our friends. Our friends elect us to the congress of complacency, then exile us for the public discovery that we are real. It is possible that no one became a realist who was not first carried up to this Tarpeian rock upon the shoulders of one's fellows.

The positive function of the masses upon the individual: silently to revere strength so much that once a man has acquired the right to this reverence they have at last the need to tear it back out of him ... and this makes him stronger.

The question sets the trajectory of the answer. The crowd stands safely behind. If the crowd has aimed the canon askew, I can only lose: if I answer, my answer will be set off in vain ... if I refuse to answer, I have "avoided the battle" ... if I stop to debate the positioning of the question itself, there will be no crowd pleasing thunder ... if I seize the question and turn it round, correctly aiming at the problem — the crowd — I will be torn to pieces.

Could it be that we were thus selected by nature? That the human is the highest *possible* creature? The fact that ten humans united by a "cause" were ... *are* stronger than the highest, most refined species *possible* has perhaps devalued our planet ... but we protect ourselves from such belittling discoveries by banding together and surrounding the bastard.

The Error-Making Organ

Given enough time we would find a lack of pain as unendurable as the predominance of pleasure.

Object **A** falls with great velocity. Object **B** falls slowly. From the perspective of Object **A**, Object **B** *rises* ... reason why after we fall from a lofty religious experience, the idea of "mind" or "metaphysics" remains seductive.

59

If I had no memory, would the cue ball move the eight ball? Are "cause" and "effect" only *human* interpretations whose only "existence" lies with the human brain? Likewise, how can we have *meaningful reflection* without memory? Is *meaning,* then, a convenient error? A sedative for reality?

60

We laugh at ourselves and our foolishness, for until now we had thought that "meaning" was a need, an undernourished organ of human nature, and when we found it impossible to satisfy "our need," we found a name for this *absence* of meaning, *"nothingness."* In reaction, we even thought on occasion that this vacuum was the goal. At last we had a voice to sound out the depths of our souls ... and with great success, for we had become hollow.

61

Sometimes I feel as though I am the last to get the joke — and it took me an inordinately long time just to crack a smile. Now I look around me and find no one else chuckling. But the humor is so obvious to me that I cannot presume to be the first among my acquaintances to have laughed out loud. It can only be that everyone else has, once again, found something more serious than existence.

62

Sometimes the illusion yields to the reality and sometimes the reality yields to the illusion. So to which do I hold fast? Whichever makes me stronger at the given moment. The essential thing is to remember that the one always returns to the other. On the other hand, the suggestion here that reality and illusion *want to meet* is not evident to me. That they *want to collide* is rather the case.

63

I take my observations at face value, but their conclusions depreciate.

64

Out of hunger, we swoop down from the idea, and snatch up our prey, lift it back to our heights ... and find ... just another idea.

65

An idea is not a creation, but an object knocked out of place by another object and made obvious by the threat of disorder. We round it off to shape and fit it into a familiar environment again ... to hide the danger. This repression and falsifying, this chipping off certain pieces and allowing others to remain we wrongly call the "idea." To grasp the matter more fully we would have to include the confusion.

66

Vanity: How the mighty hunter caught a snake with his ankle.

67

The mind is not more than the sum of its parts. In fact, if we were all-knowing, mind would show itself to be much less ... since human vanity would have no place in the equation.

The question is not *"Is the whole greater than the sum of its parts?"* (For the answer is a disheartening *"No."*) But *"Is a human greater than the sum of the senses?"* And the answer is *"Yes,"* but not to the relief of our fears, for that *something else* is diet, culture, habit, heredity ... Indeed, the next question seems to be whether or not the whole is lessened by our finding nothing amiss.

The third thing: Water is part hydrogen and part oxygen and that third thing? ... one part human.

As the cloud of metaphysics floats away, we see only this small, delicate mechanism which operates beyond our capacity for explanation ... and it is its simplicity which baffles us. We are tempted to call it *free will*, but that too floats away. We would call it *determinism*, but that would offend us.

The Chess Player: We celebrate the fallibility of the computer, but only as long as its human origins remain concealed.

I am incorrigible. I would have every object of the universe mechanically predictable but myself.

The greatest threat to self-mastery lies in the testimony of successful people. Where there is fortune there is an excess of vanity and where there is vanity there is "cause and effect" ... all reasons twisted smugly inward ... toward the fortunate.

The second greatest threat lies in the testimony of failures. Where there is misfortune there is self-reproach and denial ... all "reasons" mangled and pointing everywhere.

74

I do not despair for lack of meaning, but for lack of *increase*. It is *decreasing* that forces the question of futility upon me. Upon a sudden and incredible *increase* I do not have enough words for the meaning of life: its wonder is too great for me, yet I gratify myself in the attempt anyway. I reason backwards and reconstruct a flattering chain of events, all of them "causes" of my success ... all previous events and "attributes," good and bad, redeemed in this one unspeakable moment of victory.

And yet all has been reversed ... all a rationalization of the egotist. Every thought has run ahead, like an excited boy marching in front of a victory parade ... every word inverted before a vanity mirror ... so that in disaster one looks at the world for the first time without this mirror ... and all is a cryptic, meaningless tangle of arguments.

75

I am sure of the world. Then one day the tide of fortune ebbs and I find all the braces to my life on one side only.

76

The *infinite* is too much for me to understand or use, but the thought of a smaller universe crushes me.

77

He climbs the ship's ladder faster than the ship sinks ... and feels proud of himself ... up to his neck and still bragging.

Habits are invisible and effortless and therefore dangerous. As the decadent habit bores away at one's hull, one neither feels nor hears anything ... and can only console oneself as the ship goes down with a resignation to one's "Fate."

Another danger: a single bad habit has wound itself so tightly into a thousand strands of good habits that one senses only the braided whole ... and concludes that only the tonsure can save.

Another difficulty lies in the intricate makeup of the universe and the flow of time: "cause and effect" itself becomes a riddle. One can not see clearly enough ... does not have an organ to see all of the contributions to an "action" ... yet how readily, almost eagerly, do we hold ourselves accountable ... how we reason backwards toward shame or pride. Never mind that we cannot see far enough down the paths of our own histories ... never mind that what little we *do* see is cut up by the woven shadows of other events ... somehow we have managed to conjure up "intent" ... *with proof!*

Often one feels a tremor without seeing anything at all ... not merely a subconscious tremor which can be coaxed out and understood, but a collision of invisible, alien fates with histories which precede all observers. As in a collision of two ice bergs, one feels the tremor, but from tip to tip the distance is so great and there is so much sea and fog between them that one is truly confused as to what has just happened.

One of the ice bergs may even break up, ground into pieces between several older and harder mountains of ice, leaving some observers with a sense of victory and others with defeat.

This is how a man wakes up one day and congratulates himself while another gnashes his teeth, simply because each found himself atop his own berg when the two collided. They do not really understand why or how it happened but take what little they have seen thus far *for all that has happened thus far* ... concluding with some personal quality that gratifies and blames or to a metaphysical truth that rationalizes the event into something explainable and safe.

80

The habitual contact with a stimulus (or collective stimuli) plus the subject's inevitable reaction(s) create what I call a *drive*. This drive becomes weaker when the stimulus is kept at a distance over time, most effectively when severed from all sensory contact. Each move toward the stimulus increases the force of this river ... and each move away adds another brick to the dam of this now undiverted energy.   The drive weakens.   The river lowers. However, the spring of energy remains, and having no channel in which to pour, its force accumulates.   That is to say, the tendency toward a particular response has decreased in direct proportion to the increase in the potential for a response to *any* stimulus which might happen to show itself — whether that be the reintroduction of the old stimulus or the introduction of a new one.

On the one hand, the subject now has a deep, empty riverbed into which many other tributaries are still pouring ... while the main body of water, behind the dam, accumulates a tremendous reserve of force ... until the dam finally bursts, the *force* eroding the original river to greater depths or spilling over the banks and creating a whole new course ... becoming a new river that deserves a new name.   That is to say, he drudges up deeper reasons for his previous tendencies or he is compelled to make contact with the most available and gratifying series of stimuli ... smug in the pursuit of a new "line of reasoning."

81

Searching for a Black Tack on a Black Wall: A human is a creature who makes things disappear through repeated contact. After living on a ship for a month, the sailor has accustomed himself to the waves of the sea. Within his sensory world, it is as if the rolling and pitching have ceased. Then this creature goes ashore and nearly falls down because it is the land that now pitches and moves: it is a movement that now exists *as an*

29

absence of movement ... and only as such can it be "sensed."

A question: how can I see forces which affect me *without the cessation of these forces?* ... or create an environment where I am at least thrown out of synchronization with these forces? Perhaps even now there is a key force, a stimulus, a recurring event, with which I am, through ceaseless contact, unable to "perceive" and therefore unable to put to my advantage or remove as an obstacle. If so, there seems to be no end to the forces I take for granted ... nor an end to my ingratitude ... just as there seems to be no end to the *seduction of these "invisible" forces: I want them to serve as the basis for a "world beyond" ... as a means of escape.*

Or, am I already at the end. Nothing is hidden after all. This is just my first encounter with a "corner" of the knowable universe, and I am too stubborn and disappointed to turn away.

82

That which produces hand movement is the same as that which produces these words ... *and it is not "consciousness."* When I *"tell"* my feet to move gracefully, in any motion approaching a dance, I cannot honestly say that I am consciously controlling my feet. Consciousness, in fact, gets in the way ... trips up the dance. Consciousness, rather, races from behind ... catches up to the aftermath ... *and takes all of the glory.*

83

The problem of "Truth" is not half so useful as a little observation. Unfortunately, "Truth" is twice as interesting. Our problem solving faculty, we observe, is one of our problems.

84

Once in a while, a bad dream: in the end one is not free, just vain ... and that to wake up from this vanity is to find oneself falling from a great height. Freedom, here, is only time to reflect ... with nothing to push against or grab onto ... freedom no longer as a struggle toward something, but as a frantic squirming toward the best posture for impact ... at most, freedom as learning to sleep well again.

The Irreducible Surface

85

There is a point where Logic loses control ... in precisely the same way in which there is a height beyond which a building will fall.

86

Nature never makes a mistake, despite all our hopes and efforts.

87

We are here because we have suffered misfortune or failed everywhere else, yet here we find ourselves alone, at last, with our first real victory — not because we are stronger or wiser than others but because there are no others here.

88

Upon the surface of things we do not see anything of value other than our explanation. We grope along each new path in life, until our explaining becomes habitual and our eyes seem a hindrance to insight.

89

One feeds the institutionalized with stories and maxims. But in the quest toward real satisfaction one must stop listening and start watching. Let one's eyes follow the bread; where it disappears, there is need.

90

To say that we are finally content with the superficial betrays our disappointment ... implies that *what we lost* had been esteemed at greater value. We placed our highest bid on the illusion, but *settled* for reality. Only humans measure in this way: our cherished illusions tipping the scales against our reality.

91

In life, as in the kernel of wheat, much of the value lies in the shell, yet everyone wants to show me the "inner" world of man ... to feed me the husked "essence" of experience, and I am to be satisfied today to the same extent that I will be malnourished tomorrow.

92

Some quasi-humans crawl through life as miners of the soul only because they have never stood up to see themselves against a fostering background ... or at least not long enough to feel upon the body the influences of the immediate world: people, objects, perspective, smells, sounds, digestion, metabolism ... The mishap in the evolution of our species is that our background teaches us that there is something *"inside"* ... something *"under the surface"* — and so we burrow after it, neglecting our grip upon our surface reality in order to dig toward shiny little *ideas*. Perhaps one day we may even pierce through one side of our dark mountain, stand up in the cloud of our own dust, blinded by the light of the sun and choking in the purity of the air. We are repulsed and thus further convinced that the superior, healthy *reality* lies within that dark tunnel and toward the "soul," for we can see something shiny just a few paces ahead ... and our forehead ... it seems to glow and lead us on.

An eye for nothingness: Let's admit it. We no longer believe in God, but we search on for *something like Him,* for *something like eternity* ... *in vain.* And nature, as they say, hates a vacuum and threatens to fill this one with the superficial. *"Anything but this!"* we shout and guard the vacuum with our lives.

94

My reality is only as valuable as it is final. What am I saying! ... it is only as *real* as it is final.

95

Even if the water *were* deep, we still could not see beyond our reflections.

96

Each time a truth falls from my night sky, it streaks across my horizon in a flame of wonder. This falling too is not Truth, but wonder; the heart beats faster at the sight. Our night is full of stars, fixed and persistent, but somehow we find ourselves wishing upon those which fall.

Perhaps our worst suspicions hereby prove themselves. We are no longer dangerously close to contradiction but already suffering from the collision with actuality: there are no truths, only lies ... and this itself cannot be Truth ... and we suddenly realize that we are standing in a doorway, mumbling and waving our arms before our closest friends.

Are we then fools after all? Caught in our own flames of wonder, our hearts rising, but only because we are falling?

Our universe has become insecure, and with that insecurity, that rare moment of hazard and riot, one is exhilarated ... with what? Some beast had plucked out our hearts and threw them up before our eyes, and before this realization brought us to our knees, we found our hearts remained in our breasts, beating stronger than before ... the thrill of the whole universe, again, contained in a single human organ ... the entire universe, again, felt as one.

What!? ... to have another possibility! ... but now we must withdraw from our friends to make our newest wish, for we feel our oldest suspicions again ... that we are, for all our efforts, isolated human events ... fools with a flair for the grandiose.

97

Concluding with the Surface: The "mind" is a fly in a jar. As long as it respects its limits, remains in the center, it can see far and clear and feel its freedom, but as soon as it tries to fly "beyond" its reality ... tries this angle and that ... to get "behind" the fact ... beneath the surface ... "in the world but not of the world" ... as soon as it flies off in a buzzing fury toward the *"ultimate,"* we hear nothing but the frenzied pit-pat of its own scared ideas. Do not misunderstand me here. To be the fly in the jar is not the despair, but quite the contrary, to be the fly *and believe that there is no jar* is the madness. We need not transcend reality — *reality is the goal* — we must transcend *"mind"* ... to see through the glass but never forget that it is there.

The Written Attempt

Why I use aphorisms: I have no chart or destination. I can only *correct* my course. I sail against the wind, tacking against each discovered error. At most I have only a tendency to behave in a certain manner, and I have altered my course so many times that I would not dare calculate a destination based upon my present direction, so forgive my methods here. If I could put together a treatise on the course and destination of my efforts, I would. As it is, I can only record each correction as it occurs.

When one comes upon a stimulus which promotes confusion, do we stop to sort out the confusion? If one takes a hallucinatory drug and if this drug presents the user with a problem, does one then feel obligated to take the drug again tomorrow, in order to solve that problem? Perhaps. But if one has made the attempt day after day, and if one is so lucky as to have a few sober moments, ought one not to conclude, after so many failures, that the problem itself is a hallucination? ... the solution being to abstain from the hallucinatory agent? ... my case against book-induced solutions to human problems.

Let me face it squarely: I fear death. I do not like the ugly things in life. Moreover, I may write because I can do nothing else.

And this is the first obstacle that I find in my way: am I perhaps seeking, not a new way to live, but a consolation?

Much of the great literature in the world seems to be merely a compensation for the author having failed in some ambition ... a lifelong attempt to justify oneself, "I'm better off this way."

102

To think without writing: to face the same mountain of ice every day ... simply because I will not use ropes.

103

Waiting for thoughts to leap out and letting the idea govern its own length, leaves one with a clean conscience ... as opposed to writing a long, calculated essay, where point after point must be compromised in order to fit into a logical whole.

What should we have learned two thousand years ago? That the gulf between who I am and who I imagine myself to be is exactly as wide as the gulf between a collage of observations and a reconciled system.

104

I am as yet unknown ... invisible ... and it is only through the needle of my experience and the pigment of my words that I can at least make an illustration of myself.

Yet this man says my illustrations are crude and in poor taste. But what do I care of beauty and taste when, until now, I could not be seen at all.

105

I have no spontaneity. I am not pouring out from a center of nothingness. On the contrary, I am trying to fill that very emptiness.

We perform surgery on the living language, and it dies on the table. We work and work feverishly to bring it back to life. We give it up for dead and bury it without ceremony. It rises again, untimely, as a crude monstrosity of hunger and revenge. It is here at our home again, screaming out vulgarities and pounding fiercely upon our door. What have we done? What have we done?

107

An aphorism is never my focus. My focus is more like the steel blade that I press to the grindstone. The sparks that fly off, spectacular and brief, get all of the attention.

108

A goal: A book must not become an attempt to point toward humor, wit, style, or the idea behind the fact. Each sentence must point toward mechanical force in the mechanical world. In the end, something in the immediate world must *move.* Of itself, a book ought to be nothing more than a handbook to the engine of existence, so that one is encouraged to set the book aside in order to pick up the wrench.

109

A caution: Once a writer leaves the immediate world and begins to throw ideas onto the page, he can rearrange key words at random and still feel like he has said something meaningful.

110

I would have every thought stoop and touch the Earth but that I already know the impossibility of the effort. A thought seems to have a mind of its own and would rather leave itself open to flattering interpretations.

A work of art, like the artist, is only as strong as it stands alone ... only as rich as that which *it makes its own.*

112

On dangerous books: Sometimes I read, not to discover a beneficial influence, but to free myself from the requirements of a stronger existence, a reading which keeps all of the more difficult choices just out of reach.

113

It is not that I want to read so few books; it is just that *I refuse to learn* from those same few books those very lessons which experience teaches me much later. All of my reading pours through me as if I were a sieve. Once in a rare while a word knots up with an event and plugs the mesh. I manage to retain a little more in my small pool of wisdom. Certain books promote this knotting and clogging phenomenon more than others. I have no choice but to limit my reading to them.

114

There is no writer so great he cannot be done without.

The Turning Point

An attempt to find a positive orientation toward life which does not deny reality

115

The proud mind denies the existence of the stimulus in an argument, and so does not see or feel the force of the necessary response, creating the illusion that it is not the perceiver but the world that is twisted.

The Nature of this Book and Some of its Problems

116

This is not a book which proceeds from point *A* to point *B*. I am more concerned with the *natural phenomenon* of "spontaneity." I need to stress the words *"natural phenomenon."* The words "transcendence" and "spontaneity" are too frequently excuses for flights *away* from reality ... so I like to temper such words with the acknowledgment that spontaneity and transcendence are governed by natural laws and that they are limited to the private human experience; they are not "supernatural forces" or external "authorities" to which I must appeal. I am not afraid to disinfect the misunderstanding of both realists and escapists alike by sponging the issue with the behaviorist's word-set ... while preserving the *exalted sensation* as a goal. I am also not afraid of *my* life, my direct experience with my small reality being of more importance and of greater validity than all of the greatest literature combined. I need not appeal to another "thinker" before making the attempt to live. I live. That is enough.

I also make it a habit to record my spontaneous moments, however inconsistent and unrelated one discovery might be from another. Through categorization, these particular experiences grow back towards a *"whole."* It is a method of *discovering* the conclusion, not one of inventing a "conclusion" first and then working toward that invention. In short, I establish the means and let the ends appear when it will ... as it will.

From my own personal angle, I do not necessarily deal with the topic of spontaneity as much as it is my attempt, outside of the writing experience, to create the set of circumstances which brings about the *moment of spontaneity as often as possible ... and simultaneously to be in a position to record the event ... as it occurs.* Although this is an *end*, it is also an attempt to look over my shoulder at the *means* which brought about this *end*. This has proven to be a much more difficult task than I at first imagined it would be. It does feel a lot like magic ... or a divine influence.

However I maintain a deep faith in material reality. I am confident that every cog and wheel of the "mind" can be uncovered. Personal science ... *a self-behaviorism*, if you will, and that strong, unjustified respect for the sensation of dignity are our first steps toward "becoming" ... toward increased self-worth ... *living*.

Now perhaps I am ready to defend my unwillingness to write a book which proceeds from point *A* to point *B*. Imagine the "intentional" act of running from point *A* to point *B*. I am an athlete, let's say; I have a line behind which I stand, and I can see another line in front of me exactly one hundred meters away. The gun goes off. I stay in my lane and race to the finish. I win or I lose. If I am the average person, then I am happy or sad as a consequence of whether I have won or lost. This book is not of that nature.

The runner from point *A* to point *B* has also, simultaneously, arrived at point *C* — from the point of view of *becoming*. His muscles have grown stronger; his coordination has improved; his reflexes have quickened. Every race completed improves his ability to reach point *B* with greater and greater proficiency. This improvement ... this point *C* is what this book is about, and it is dependent upon a single natural law to which we are so accustomed that we can no longer see: *repetition.* Consider this book then, not as *the* race from point *A* to point *B*, but as a thousand races, run solely with the intent of tracing the tendency toward point *C* ... or, to use another word-set, toward a legitimate spirituality.

I will admit to several other problems with this book, chiefly, that of categorization. The book is in continual flux. A thought arrives to contradict a previous thought. Or, a previously categorized thought is suddenly *re*-categorized under a very different heading. Reading the book this month and reading the updated version next month show two different books ... two different authors. Yet, in my own defense, what is regarded as a failure in the book can be a consequence of the author's *becoming* ... an advance ... and therefore, a personal success.

If I am to have any claim to honesty, I cannot easily discard behaviorism ... nor the testimony of my five senses, nor the store of experience in the memory. I cannot use fear, social necessity, or ignorance as "proofs" of a God or of another world.

Within this sobering realism, my effort is to redeem my human experience, and, to say it again, not to try to escape from it by proposing a reality "beyond" this one. I am fully aware that the word "redeem" implies that I begin from a sense of worthlessness. In the past, I have been justly accused of not being "positive enough." I can only say in a feeble attempt at a defense that the positive ... *cheerful* outlook on *this* life is my goal. However, if today's attempt proves to be impossible, am I then to go back to sleep or to tell lies? In a stronger defense of my outlook on life, I will say that I have perhaps found some hints of a *genuine* joy in *this* life: the aforesaid *moments of growth* ... the exhilaration of those moments ... and also the act of recording those moments *as they occur.* There are times when I feel I have achieved a solid victory or two in this regard. Let the reader be the judge.

Another problem is that I should perhaps have waited until the book was "finished" — when I have found a "*more* positive" outlook and when my observations have found their "final place" within the book's organic development. Yet if the reader fully understands the process from which I begin, then that reader will also understand that the book will never be finished until I have passed on ... or have at least been incapacitated by misfortune. I need to grow ... that remains of greater importance than stopping in an attempt to make a "final statement." And so, as premature as it is, with this need *not* to finish, that is to say, *to continue growing* ... and also to *exhibit* that process of growing, *through that very process*, I present the next stage of my "book."

The Impossible Realist

117

One day I woke up and everyone I had ever met was either a fool or a liar ... another day, much later, I found that this was the first real step toward myself.

118

The next question is not, "Can we live *in spite of* our awareness of our condition?" nor, "Would it be better to go back to sleep?" but, "Can we live *by* this awareness?"

119

What is depth? To the surface of things I am converted. That all else is illusion I am sure. It even seems now that my *soul* is only as deep as my grip on the shallow is unrelenting. *"This is my reality,"* I remind myself. *"I will never let go. Given the chance, I will grasp for more!"*

120

I now see that my *immediate realism* may be just as much of a blunder as that *idealism* which places thought in a "reality *beyond* this world."

This section is an important tack, in the nautical sense, against what I call the "surface," that reality which is only immediate and does not include "repetition."

This is a very difficult and hazardous attempt to sail against a violent wind. Please do not imagine that I am rejecting the physical world. I am not rejecting the immediate reality; rather, I assert that our "immediate reality" is a consequence of human perception. More importantly, I assert that there are additional, simultaneous, and *equally* valid perceptions on our *total* reality. (Again, I am not trying to set up the Metaphysical Universe here or paint a door onto a prison wall. I am speaking only in terms of *physical* perception.)

As a metaphor, consider the following: The left eye sees from one angle and the right eye from another. They both look upon a single object, however, and the brain somehow manages to unify the separate perspectives into "one mental object" so perfectly that we rarely make note that we are using two separate perspectives. And this dual perspective yields us a sense for depth in our world. Just so, our multiple perspectives on reality yield us a sense for "meaningfulness" ... although we are rarely aware that we are bringing multiple perspectives into a single instance.

In short, my "spiritual turning point" is a confession that an important variable has been left out of my human equation.

122

It may very well be true that we are only realists of the *immediate* in the hope that it might bring us prestige. Were there no acclaim for the written word perhaps we would even stop thinking. Forgive me. I cannot help but wonder what it could be that would send someone toward this forsaken viewpoint.

We could say that the skin is the end of *"my self,"* or, as some like to fancy, that *"I"* am further *inward.* If I lop off an arm, for example, *"I"* still am. But if one proceeds in this manner, parsing the definition down to the "core," so to speak, one will end up with nothing, and then of course one has to write a book about it: "Nothingness and *(add any word here)."* But *whatever it is that we are* it cannot be found *inwardly. Outwardly* is closer to the truth. There is much of me that exists beyond my skin. While reflecting upon such matters, who would dare say that *glass* was the end of the mirror?

"I wish nothing. I hope nothing. I believe nothing — yet the surface of my world shimmers with beauty." Let this be my declaration of independence.

A thorough skeptic is one who denies the possibility of a starting place — but nonetheless finds it impossible to act accordingly. Indeed, I never found a skeptic so thorough that he would go hungry due to his inability to prove the reality of the menu. And just like the rest of us, the skeptic still ranks authors according to their worth and makes his purchases accordingly. He scans the newspaper for a good movie and then proceeds toward the cinema with an unconscious confidence that all will proceed as anticipated. The laboratory rat, too, sniffs and "knows" full well that the cheese has been pressed once again in that self-same corner, and he sets off with an unconscious confidence that all will proceed as before ... that is to say, *as anticipated.*

However, when it comes to *philosophical conversation,* competing stimuli are neglected because they are of "no importance" — stimuli which set up a desire this moment, then knock it down in the next — which have our philosopher, who plans out his ascent up the mountain of knowledge, sliding down a mud hill without a word to say in his own defense. He draws his conclusions accordingly: "philosophical knowledge" is ineffective. He has now been reconditioned into a *thorough skeptic*. Humorously, he does not see the behavioral influence but still takes pride in the fact that he has indeed debunked the *primacy* of logic. Ironically, he implies the very *primacy* of logic in his own mind with his *constant* debunking of "logic as starting place" *by way of logic* ... a *primacy* betrayed by his very unwillingness to look elsewhere.

In short, *his* skepticism still ignores behavioral reality. Consequently, *his* knowledge is indeed ineffective. His certainty "that no logical philosophy can have a legitimate starting place" evidently does not stop him from *wanting* to discuss the matter. "Pride in debunking" is his wedge of cheese, by which he *wants* this logical maze. This is the paragon of nine-to-five philosophers. What a perfect little mouse he is who loves his cheese so much that he will run the maze again and again *to prove that it is just a maze* ... but never realizing that he at the same time proves he is just a mouse *by his inability to see how or why he wants the maze.* Consequently, he sees not a single, convenient piece of day-to-day behavior. Diet, as far as he is concerned, has no value next to his one and only "certainty of logical impossibility."

That one should pursue such a thorough skepticism at the expense of tactical wisdom is indeed an interesting case. The solution is one of stimulus management ... *generalship*, where a thousand desires are marshaled toward a single victory like so many drilled soldiers under Caesar. Yet the thorough skeptic turns an ear to his untried advisor at precisely that moment where his own eyes are required most ... at the moment of a battle which he thought too small to be considered a *"battle."* He stayed, he listened, he blundered.

126

A responsible skeptic does not say, "Here is the abyss." A responsible skeptic says, "Here is the undeniable abyss. Is there not something affirmative and substantial in the fact that I am here as its observer. *I think and therefore I am."* Yes, and I can even say, *"I do not think and therefore I am."* Or, *"I am not and therefore I am."* To think, to utter, to lie, to renounce oneself ... all bear witness that some part of me, however feeble and error-prone, *participates* with that abyss. Thus, the *ability* to posit the nothingness of my existence proves its substance. That I *can* and *do* assume is more substantial than any possible assumption.

127

We exist only within paradox. That is the condition of our existence. We acknowledge the absolute reality of the *immediate* world but must reflect to do so. Our reflections are rendered "meaningless" when dismantled again into immediate realities. In fact our reflections are only as rich in wonder and meaning as they are far from our immediate reality. Yet, our distance ... our singular response as conditioned by a multitude of previously received reinforcements ... *our "totaled immediate reality"* accounts for both the surface and the depth, the stark reality and the meaning of this very observation we are making in this very paragraph.

128

A rigorously grounded logic — a harsh grip upon *surface reality* — is a stale biscuit: we cannot deny its ability to sustain us through difficult times, but we rarely find ourselves *that* desperate.

129

As I grow more and more certain of my surface world, I cannot deny this new shimmer on the surface ... and it is not a "faith in things unseen," not "the unknown god," nothing "beyond" ... but a hope rises up alongside an unyielding method.

I know I have fathered this delicate creature. She is dressed in white and steps out from the shadows of the chapel. I dance with her for the last time, bravely.

46

130

Within the human experience of *the real*, there are no *real* prisons, since we always have this one, *horribly meaningless* door which in times of peace we deny, avoid, or refuse to talk about ... while in dire emergency — for example, when we understand reality to the point of claustrophobia — we find ourselves laughing hysterically through the legitimacy of the exit.

131

The human experience remains unexplained, not because the species lacks an organ efficient enough for the task. On the contrary, it is because he is too proficient in the art of explanation. He often holds this tool up so close to the eyes that he blots out the greater part of experience.

132

The remedy for the error prone "mind" is not the amputation of the "higher faculties." On the contrary, this error-making organ, once it ceases to take itself too seriously, can actually lend a hand in the redemption of everything petty. But first it must see through itself.

133

Two "realists" can hold a conversation and soon it becomes evident that they are only disappointed mystics, trying to console themselves for that "something more" they had lost ... no thought whatsoever toward how far they should or could carry "realism" ... no thought that realism could *yield control* and *promote advance* ... or drown us.

134

If physiological reality could be seen as a scale, within which one may have more or less force, more or less joy from existence, then

I would say that certain orientations toward reality elevate; others, send us downward. This is my objection to modern realists. In the process of building their perspective, they give no thought for *their own* physiological reality. That is, the physiological perspective is, as it were, more akin to a glass elevator[*] than a duck blind. Ignoring the physiological flux of the observer does not bring one closer to *disinterested objectivity.* Rather, such ignorance precludes the goal. Yet as descendants of the ascetic order the realists have acquired the habit of resignation, and so they resign all to a single, myopic honesty. They travel up and down the whole scale of possible heights and depths, sitting in the corner, cursing their fate or rejoicing their fortune ... never seeing that realism is a human invention .... that any claim for "objective observation" implies *man as machine* ... and so why not care for the fuel, the gears, or a *real* steering mechanism? Rational Idealism refuted, why continue to believe we *intend* our actions by way of our thoughts?

[*]The presence here, of an elevator and its artificial control panel, may seem in poor taste. I will agree that it is a poor choice as a "poetic" metaphor, but I will also argue that the whole descent toward realism — like spiritual elevation — is artificial — is like a "building" in that it is an addition to nature. The building opposes nature in the sense that it is raised up in opposition to the laws of gravity, erosion ... etc. In short, the realist's perspective must be trained.

Personal Science

135

Realist: The word means so many things to so many different people that it should never be used without the utmost care. Nevertheless, one might rashly put up the word now and then as a farmer puts up a scarecrow, in the hope that ungrounded minds might fly elsewhere.

136

The farmer already *does* what the botanist does not yet *"know."* This does not make the botanist inferior, but it certainly does not leave the world hungry with waiting either.

137

How far I carry Realism: "I would take the full brunt of your argument but that I cannot endure halitosis. It is for this more beautiful world and its pure air that I surrender my right to a rebuttal. You may take this as a victory, but take it in silence."

138

Knowing the answers is not nearly as valuable as knowing the art of finding answers.

139

When we see that an argument is at the same time *a stimulus*, then clarity of thought begins.

I struck with my hardest hammer against my hardest reality, and the world, in response, began to ping. Soon I could hear music ... took delight in the ring. I even began to sing along, and the embarrassment would have overtaken me if I were not saved by the upturned corner of my lip, for I take my smirk as evidence.

141

Where everyone says "wisdom" I can say "personal science." Where everyone says spirit I can say "blood." Nothing will be lost.

142

The difference between me and the behaviorist: I have more data. I rob this We-science and add the plunder to the verified data of the Me-science.

Another difference: well, I have a knack for the art of life ... that is, I, unlike science, can appropriate goals.

143

If I truly want the experimental life, I must be willing to isolate myself as specimen.

144

The first goal of a philosophy should be sobriety ... so that one can more accurately engineer the next exploit.

145

When reality interferes with my life: In the daily transactions between my two economies — the mundane business of life and that of my pleasant dreams — I must have a competent manager in both companies, the object of each is to balance the books at the end of each day. I also must not permit the one to grasp for "more" than is necessary. I do not want the one to acquire too much debt with the other ... nor to lend too much. The one needs the other's future business.

146

Without wonder life would become something that had to be endured ... a succession of petty, meaningless tasks. On the other hand, without an eye for the superficial, I could never steer an event, never become anything more than an accident ... never worthy of anything, and life would become just an endurance of disappointments.

147

Dreams are the stuff of life? Very well, but one would do well to know that things are the stuff of dreams. So where does that leave us? ... with a little more control.

148

We are bored with reality: It's ironic that most of those who discuss "causation" do not regard the discussion itself as an effect, and would rather "get on with the matter" when we try to introduce the topic: "Which breakfast would increase our ability to discuss this topic?"

149

Real change is never as precise or smooth as we would like it to be. We soon find that our carefully drawn blueprints and our precision instruments no longer apply. We pick up a rock, screw up our faces and pound.

150

Working toward control over human nature is something like applying wrench and screwdriver to a machine whose wheels and fans are spinning so fast that they appear stationary or nonexistent. We begin with confidence and then ...

151

If there is but one cup of control for the entire ocean of force, I want it.

152

With self-control, the goal is not to *resist desire* (temptation) but to *control what one desires*.

153

Proving control and taking control are different matters. Better to leave the former to future research, which is dependent upon the acquisition of the latter.

154

Our necessary error: That we cannot explain nor prove our control does not take it away from us. *That we believe we have it* is our good fortune.

155

Perhaps one can only hold oneself responsible for one's destination in old age. In youth, one's drives are so strong and full of energy that the last thing one will do is rein oneself in. Only after a few years do one's drives recede to the point where one can ... *must* seize the reins ... but as one who walks an old horse. To be the exception here ...

156

The human creature is amazingly complex for having so few tools of influence. And this flatters us: we would rather sift through our complexities than apply a single tool to ourselves. We would rather be "free" than have any degree of real control. A simple fact can send a man whimpering to his knees begging for the illusion to take him back — something as simple as "Man is a machine."

157

First nature or second nature? But no one has a right to this question today. We are all rules that want to become exceptions. All nature is bound, but we want our "freedom." That second nature we wear in public and swear by ... what is that but the hair shirt which rubs our skin raw? ... our first nature, not *outgrown*, but too sore to move.

158

I want control, not the badge of control. And what do I do with control? I spend it all, and soon I have none. But what *ought* I to do? Pursue greater control. Why? To accumulate strength and force. Why? To pursue greater control ...

159

He who seeks control usually does so in a violent storm, because he *must* have it. Suppose he gains control. He would blunder then if he thought that control were only possible in storms, since that would confuse *the need for something* with *the thing itself.* Control is calm. And one gains it or does not gain it ... storm or no. But how many people, having found a degree of control in danger, pursue greater and greater dangers without first testing control? ... and why? ... because such a *real* victory would have neither excitement nor spectator.

Resentment

160

Resentment may have less to do with other people than we think. The feeling that one has been cheated becomes inescapable with those who continually empty themselves in the belief that this is how one becomes full.

161

There is a bog where the mud is knee deep. Around the edge of this bog there is dry ground. If I go around, is this cowardice or self-respect? Easy enough to answer.

Now, consider the same situation but where my worst enemy stands up to his knees in the middle of this bog, taunting me. Now, if I go around, is this cowardice?

No ... as long as I lay the groundwork of the former example before I confront the morass of the latter ... as long as I know that cleanliness *is* the victory ... that the question itself can be dirty ... that one conquers in this way, like a clever general, *by going around.*

162

Can a cause be just *and harmful?* I wanted to become *A* but was told that my kind are barred from serving as *B*. I am outraged and struggle my whole life to overcome the political and social obstacles and finally become *B*. In fact, I am the first of my kind ever to become *B*.

My cause is just, and I am victorious, *but I have now become the wrong person* and remain unsatisfied: the pursuit of justice was a way of indulging the spoiled child of resentment. The child demanded precisely that which had been refused and threatened to set the whole house on fire if unsatisfied ... but left unattended that smaller, weaker embryo, *my inherited and privileged task ...* which is now just a bedridden, cranky old man.

163

We do not want a fair fight. We want victory. If we are demanding a fair fight, maybe we should reconsider the whole affair, since only those with disadvantages appeal to fairness.

164

My demand for a level battlefield is an admission that I have a weaker position than my opponent ... that I resent his superiority. But what else can I do? And besides, it is this rabid disease, resentment, which does, in its own crude way, level the field already: his sobriety is no match for my raging cause.

Now I have gained the upper hand at last but am too infected to enjoy my newfound superiority. I march down from my advantage. I banish kings and with them, their wars and victories, and in their place I crown my former cause. In the name of justice, to protect the meek, that is to say, *to vent my resentment*, I scour the countryside, slaughtering every child born of high rank.

165

If we removed resentment from the argument, we could not say, "put yourself in my place," or "if this had happened to a woman" — since all appeals to fairness themselves hinge upon resentment. No, if we removed resentment from the argument, the argument itself would be in danger of vanishing. Nothing would be there ... only debris that we could have sailed on through if we had only kept our heads up. Instead we laid anchor before the wreckage, involuntarily conferring value upon it ... and with our stopping, new regrets and with them new resentments ... and still more debris floating in from our horizon.

166

Resentment is suffering a wrong without possessing the means for retribution.

167

The real problem with resentment is that it is always justifiable.

168

A petty life is so overwhelmed with the noble that it feels itself unworthy, unable to stand anywhere but in its shadow ... or in other cases, so humiliated, so indignant that it can do nothing but scream, set aflame — always to itself in the hope of scorching its enemy — regarding this self-destruction as "revenge" — or euphemistically as "self-sacrifice."

169

Another person has only as much depth as I concede to him. He can be a cardboard cut-out or the very God incarnate. To take conscious control of this mechanism, to be able to switch at will between perceptions of the real and the illusory serves me well. When another person proves harmful, I can say, "If I am sober, this *thing* is real and therefore meaningless and I am free of all need for retribution. *It* is a two-dimensional cardboard cut-out. I'll wait a while. Time, like the breeze, will brush *it* away." On the other hand, when someone proves congenial, I can say, "You intoxicate me without fail. Stay a while."

170

The smug: What I have I have deserved.

The resentful: What I lack they have ... and to no fault of my own.

The noble spirit: What I have or lack makes no difference whatsoever ... but rather, it is the direction I take with either of the two winds of fortune that makes all the difference. Neither the east wind nor the west wind matter, for I am northbound ... toward the possession of nobility itself and only this. Am I noble today? This is the only relevant question.

Overcoming resentment is not forgiveness. It is my knowing the wrong and the offender to be beneath my dignity. I move on and away.

Forgiveness is for family and friends. Revenge is for enemies of excellent quality. But the offenses of small people ought to be seen from the appropriate angle ... after we have climbed a little higher.

172

The object is not to forgive in spite of oneself. The object is a higher degree of *clarity*. That this state "forgives" is coincidental and accounts for the misunderstanding. To forgive or not to forgive was never the conflict. The true conflict was one of level: whether one had the strength to climb above the lower conflict, to exist from a higher point of view.

Potential

173

Genius is power of direction. It actually amounts to less power than talent or innate ability, as there are some talents so great as to be sent out of control.

174

Potential will pursue an end, at the expense of a higher end, only because one had the means at one's immediate disposal.

The problem with irrelevant potential is that one needs to feel capable and suddenly finds that here — at the juncture of decision — one is not only capable but already congratulating oneself.

176

There is a difference between asking, "What is my potential?" — and the question, "How can I elevate potential itself?"

177

An elevated purpose is often confused with that weakest point of one's existence where potential can no longer withstand breaking out.

178

There is a virtue in postponing a valuable act ... if in its place a lesser act has greater value *as a habit.* Obvious enough, yet the seduction of an immediate victory is more than the average human can withstand.

179

A possibility: One resists a victory which is merely available — resists the seduction of every cheap and easy display, knowing that the strength of its seduction lies in its availability and in a deficit of self-esteem. Such "potential" is a bubble which bursts at its weakest point, the rapid deflation of the human spirit creating the illusion of "explosive power."

The ability to *create* a goal, to resist every distraction, to hurdle cheap gratifications of pride, to regard them as obstacles and pitfalls, that too should have its claims to "potential" and "intelligence."

A Magnetic North

180

I spin the globe on my desk. North is up and south is down. To what extent my orientation to the world has been set by the ethnocentricity of Europe I cannot begin to imagine. Had America been discovered from the ports of Australia I would perhaps have to read the globe while standing on my head to see what I now see. But a responsible assumption serves me well. The need to appropriate an orientation outweighs the obligation to justify that orientation. One must begin somewhere, but do we *see* that our beginning is necessarily smug? ... that the beginning is a privilege granting too much license? ... that before our personal science begins we have already made the choice: we either affirm reality by our opposing it — as one confronts an opponent and thereby grows stronger *as a reality* — or we oppose reality with a frantic desire to fly from it and thereby ...

181

We do not roll smoothly toward *the highest* goal. In fact, we trundle over day-to-day pits and bumps that *necessarily* lower our sight away from *any* higher destination.

182

One needs a magnetic north, something to sail by ... and how many ships remain lost at sea because they know it is not a "true" north?

183

My guess: That increase in strength is always the object and that any decrease is always the obstacle.

184

The more I practice the art of high fate, the more I see that there is one thing that one must have ... strength in every sense of the word and in all events. Whatever one wants to do, whatever one *has* to do — from duty, from desire, from reckless will — one must acquire every piece of strength along the way.

185

The archer aims above and to the left but strikes the center ... so do I have a single eye on strength but strike a high fate.

186

If I use increasing strength as my standard, all habits fall within two categories: descending or ascending. There is no "in between" ... no standing; those who do not climb weaken.

187

Strength is value. That which I carry everywhere, especially into new circumstances, and which also *moves things* is of highest value. And with the strongest, things move even after death.

188

In the end, it is my strength ... not my words, not my badges, not my reputation ... but my strength that holds my head up.

189

Does *object A* rise or fall? But one must have first secured a point of reference before one can even pose the question. And in case it has not already become obvious to the reader, the point of reference I propose is *increasing strength*. Until one secures that point of reference, *object A* may not even appear to move at all.

190

What has accounted for our "strength" thus far? That tremendous force we spent on the preservation of our weaknesses.

191

Do not give me pain killers. True, I also want my existence alleviated ... but I will do so by growing stronger ... by bearing the weight of my reality.

192

The first and highest law of life: to increase. Survival is the last and lowest law, and though it is very difficult to think of survival as life, even this lowest of laws still increases me.

193

Nothing is more lacking in drama than the slow, steady habit which accumulates strength.

194

Our strength is measured by the number of times we return to that rule which necessarily increases dignity ... precisely when an exceptional humiliation urges us to the contrary.

195

Question: If increasing strength serves as my magnetic north, what then would serve as compass? Answer: My unbounded ambition ... my vanity.

196

What I seek is control, not over my destiny, but over the value of my destiny. I stand at a fork in the road and stare down each lane for as far as I can see, never considering that I have just overlooked another option available to me.

Before I choose between destination A and destination B, what would happen if I took this one step back to a prior fork in my road: Do I strive to be at a particular destination at a particular time? Or do I march by a Magnetic North, path or no path, disregarding destinations, until I am stopped?

With the former, I march toward a time and place; whom I become is secondary. With the latter, becoming is primary.

Blind Fate

197

Blind fate is the struggle to set and keep one's course according to natural dignity ... and never to be turned aside by apparent destinations, consequences, moral claims, or regret.

198

From statistic to tragedy: We can never eliminate the number of tragedies or accidents from our lives or from the world. What we can do, however, is elevate the event by keeping our error-making organ in check, thereby translating the calamity into a superior language and realizing a higher fate.

199

Maturity is best understood not as a tapering down to nothing upon the approach of old age, but with the entire conception of Past and Future stood on end, like an hour glass, where after we have allowed each day to go by, one by one, through this narrow actuality, we learn to demand less and less of the upper chamber, our future, as time passes so that we may accept more and more of the actuality toward the end. This is an improvement over our former happiness, when we looked into the upper chamber, our dreams wide and full, demanding more, always more, and caring not for experiences to the contrary as they passed into the lower chamber of our memories.

200

Memory is the *absence* of pre-existing stimuli, and especially that of repeated stimuli. We do not have the stimuli in mind when we remember; our not having it is rather the thing. In fact, sometimes we need to part with the stimulus before we can see it at all.

What happens? A stimulus burns a hole in the slate of mind and leaves a new template with which we view and re-organize the world according to our harder, more enduring past. I say "re-organize" because we must change the world to make sense of it: the world is understood only so far as it can be forced into our "templates." (A friend of mine witnessed a man rip a page out of his Bible rather than admit the existence of a God who contradicted *him*.)

How does this "memory" lend control? Can I blindly grope forward, away from the bright stimuli of the present ... construct a template for the better interpretation and organization of my future ... while having no idea whatsoever what that future will be? ... since I have no means of understanding how to make or even how to comprehend the requirements of that future except through the archaic templates of the present?

Brave or Fearless

201

One can take the fear of another and mistake the reaction within oneself for courage.

202

The occasion for cowardice increases with knowledge.

203

There is more to fear from the coward than the courageous.

204

Fear is egotistical ... as if the bee actually hated my existence more than it loved the flower behind me.

205

Ninety-nine percent of courage is "going through the motions"; that is, it is an acquired habit of resisting, brought about through unceasing squabbles with the mundane. Ninety-nine percent of cowardice is thinking the whole thing over again ... and again.

206

Every "What if?" is a cowardice ... yet as such it is the prerequisite to a genuine courage. Only then can we shout our personal *"Even if!"*

207

What we need is adequate lighting — courage, that close relative to dull-wittedness. Cowardice illuminates, without fail, but to the point that we are blinded by the brighter lights of this all too intelligent thought ... like the rabbit which stops before oncoming headlights. If we somehow manage to *move*, we then recoil from an all too lucid conscience afterward, like the human which feels it is its duty to be run over by an oncoming cultural presumption but has not the courage to hold its ground. To *fear* is to create an absurd double-bind. To *fear* is to victimize oneself with one's own intelligence. Courage would have made its stand with the word, "Duty" ... in a peal of laughter.

208

Where there is no fear there is no courage.

209

I do not *have* to do anything. I do not have to breathe if I do not want to.

210

Two people are never brave together. Every inherited task is singular in nature and each hand was made to clutch its own. On second thought, others are clutching too, calmly, firmly, and with steady voices. *Their* courage is palpable, but far from inspiring, as they clutch the coattails of that rare creature who trembles but refuses to let go of *his own*.

211

The irony of an effective courage: Can I go around?

212

Fearlessness does not necessarily entail courage. If one is intelligent enough and skilled enough one can often eliminate all cause for fear in a venture. Courage is of a different sort: it lies in those who refuse to give an inch of their own dignity yet *know* that this stand is doomed.

213

Am I a coward or am I a hero? Either badge can be sewn onto my coat. The *permanence* of victory is the thing ... and that seems to have less to do with courage than with having the resources sufficient to endure a simple strategy.

I can keep a giant at a safe distance by brandishing a needle, until he is inured with the first few pricks. Hence, if we are to be intelligent, we cannot also be *too* bold. Often the real strength of our weapon lies in the weakness of our enemy's intellect and character.

The problem is not that we are simplistic creatures governed by too few mechanisms, but that the basis of the objections to our simplicity are too often *proofs* of the assertion and not refutations. The objection always hinges on a simple fear or humiliation. However, once we dismantle our insecurities and study the parts, learn how each works together into a whole, then the complete machine, with all of its hinges, wires and circuits, appears more than complex. When it so much as walks, for example, it resembles more the flying god than that simple hinge which can only squeak when an insecurity is pulled.

Courage or wisdom? When this becomes the choice, can we not convince ourselves that pursuing wisdom is, if only within the inner sanctum of the heart, a species of courage? ... that the *common* species of courage promotes and sustains nothing but an admirable foolishness? We know full well that its claim to courage lies only in this foolishness, yet we cannot withhold our admiration! ... even when a "cowardly" prudence would have saved the day. But then it takes that higher species of courage even to *see* this prudent "victory": our knuckles white with clutching the goal and never letting go ... not even for the sensation of *heroism* as it begins to overtake *us* as well.

What determines the coward from the brave?

Whether he drops or holds onto the *immediate.*

And what does one do with the *immediate?*

One steers the entire *repetition* as one would a vessel whose cargo consisted of both the human and the human's *things.*

218

But I suppose I have to interrupt here and admit that there is no difference between the terms "Courage" and "Wisdom" ... and also that they are not so prodigious of an undertaking as previously thought ... that perhaps they fall under the name of that other obscure phenomenon, of which I still can only speak of metaphorically: timing the mind to the ticks of the surface world ... cultivating a *will* to synchronize ... tapping the cogs of the illusory to the cadence of the actual. Both "Courage" and "Wisdom" then would be a type of *yielding.*

219

The "Bold" are not as fearless as they are lazy, for they have not the patience for calculation. The "Wise" are not as cowardly as they are calculating. What would become of a boldness which was not lazy? Of a *Bold Calculation?* Of an existence which was not a spectacular explosion into chaos, but its opposite: a horrible sanity in the midst of chaos ... a strategist with enough courage to *avoid* the innumerable peripheral enemies in order to turn and march painstakingly toward the center of power ... toward actual *control* over reality.

220

Before: "I brace myself against the worst of all possible consequences."

But what is the worst? The futility of such bracing ... and how does one brace oneself against futility? We wanted strength. That is what brought us here. But now we see that we were stronger without our philosophy.

After: "I brace myself upon the stone path of my garden."

And what of the worst? That was merely philosophy, but we have something more palpable than futility ... and equally well grounded. This strawberry for example.

So what is courage? Only a shout? "Even if!" We march on ... and the only mystery remaining is the insuppressible chuckle bubbling up from our depths.

From Serf to Middle Class, the Berry Picker

221

How cheaply we could purchase another's heart: a few puffs of breath! ... but we would rather sell our grand idea of ourselves, which is to say, *we* are purchased by another's breath.

222

What am I if I am a serf who refuses to obey? And then discover after my banishment that I have no instinct for command? The king will not take me back, and I fear the next leg of my journey ... for all roads end here. I wander through the wilderness, taken aback with my new fear of freedom, whimpering and crying out for a new master to serve ... and finding none better than the one I had before. I know, I know ... I have heard it all before, but *how?* ... and *with what?* How does second nature command first nature without finding itself dispatched on a final errand?

223

Thus far I have found myself rooted in middle-class soil and have dutifully and passionately continued the battle for the leveling of all classes and cultures. However, lately, I have had a thousand modern conveniences as my servants, too much time for thinking, and much too much time for leisure. I have become bored and even begin to take on, comically enough, aristocratic airs ... and with this first step back in time, toward this banished morality, the comedy plays itself out: *"The king is dead ... the throne is vacant ... can I do this without hurting anybody?"* All in my audience split their sides with laughter as I apologize with each harmless step forward ... like a peasant of the lowest order, who still believes he must be granted the *right* to self-possession before he can claim it.

224

We are not freemen. We are not even serfs, but the shadows of serfdom. We search in vain ... carry our torches and find nothing that will burn hot and bright enough to light up our faces. And what exasperates us most is that we find no one to blame for our anger ... and we have searched everywhere. But it is here, as our flame gutters out for a lack of oil, that we come upon a leaf cool and beaded with morning dew ... something that we *consume* in a forgotten manner ... something we can finally keep down and digest ... we, the middle class with our public education ... we, the cows of social science, have at last found something pleasant to ruminate:

There is no blame. There is no merit. There is no duty. There is no value or meaning ... not because we are incapable of them but because they are fictions.

But does not this newfound contentment retain us in our roles as serfs? Does not the true king, a born conqueror, shrug his shoulders at the quenching of the human spirit? ... at the very *legitimacy* of this quenching? ... as something which merely delays the subjugation of the likes of us? What? Is he still laughing at us?!

225

To stop behaving as a slave it is equally as important to stop obeying as it is to demand the master to stop commanding. We understand this in word, but cannot leave the deed undone. We can imagine ourselves as free spirits, but not as scoundrels.

226

Only "hard workers" have a real chance for an authentic existence and high fate. Unfortunately, it is almost always the master-servant morality which produces these hard workers. When the servant finally breaks with the master, the master still maintains the language appropriate to their former ranks. For the master, the moral predicament remains unchanged. This free man has become "lazy" ... "a quitter" ... "a threat to society" ... and all of this while the free man endures the roughest labor ... struggling to stand alone and on the other side of that unbridgeable gulf between the old rank and the new.

227

We cannot both befriend our master *and* gain self-mastery, since our approach to his rank is the insult of all insults. Moreover, his rebuke will always sound off with a ring of legitimacy, while our condemnation of "power" does not defeat power, but promotes its dissipation among those of us who would otherwise be his equals. We must therefore acquire equal force before we *proclaim* equal status. Until then, we conspire with necessity.

228

This man is born a servant and plots to become master. This other man is born a master and plots to preserve and extend his realm. How can we expect their strategies to have the same structure? ... or for the two to have the same definition of dignity? ... of proper conduct? How can a spectator admire both in the same way? It is the curse of the servant that when *he* pursues an ambition he must throw off all hope of encouragement or respect.

How do we serve? We, the many, without resources to command, and who condemn ourselves for our fate ... it would do us well to remember that all humans serve. If nothing else, they serve nature. Here, even a king can overstep his authority. The real question is: do we have a perfect strategy for the *next* conquest? That is, have we applied what little resources we have in order to accumulate *more resources ... and at an optimum rate?*

Self-Appropriation

A multiple choice test: Who mediates our genius?

A)

The greats of history are our mediators: Genius is an external authority to which I must appeal. All personal conclusions must first receive authorization from these mediators before these conclusions can be considered true or false. And this is of course all in order since anyone who is anybody knows that one has no right to one's own reality. To claim the contrary is to overstep my bounds, is a symptom of megalomania, and remains contrary to what I need most, humility ... also known as, low self-esteem.

B)

The people we know best are our mediators: A Genius is a type of filing cabinet, the recognition of which is quite simple. If we meet another who has been nominated for the office of genius, we must immediately request a file and test whether the nominee can produce that file without hesitation and without any sign of concern on his brow. The file itself is of no importance. It could be anything, a date, a place or any other fact — and the more unrelated to day-to-day affairs, the more accurate will be our findings.

Another popular test: ask for a list certifying that precisely those books which we have read have also been read by the nominee. And let us not forget to mention the use of quotations! One genius, whom I witnessed with my own eyes, could cite the act and scene of any Shakespearean line quoted — even when he was not called upon to do so.

One need not tally up a score here to reach a conclusion. If the nominee does not produce the record promptly and with a smooth brow, then he can not possibly have genius.

C)   I myself am my own mediator: to be a true genius is to be a sort of inept criminal. I have to be willing to plot the crime against the great authorities and to "botch the job" when my friends catch me in the act. On the one hand, I appropriate my own relationship to my own reality; on the other hand, I leave much behind ... bring too little with me to prove what I have, for the public wants to see the loot, but I have only brought myself.

231

My goal: To lift the finger to *the act of questioning* itself.

232

No one can teach me; I can only learn.

233

Only I have the metaphor for my center.

234

What are the modern stigmata?   Sympathetic suffering ... *another's* suffering, or *distant* suffering, but always safe ... as when we wear our brows heavily at a dinner party, discussing the latest crisis sold by the news media. To do away with stigmata ... to do away with *the need to prove* our sympathetic suffering is the next task. That one privately suffers in the struggle *away* from suffering is enough to make a Buddha out of the least of us. How unholy do all stigmata appear when we sanctify ourselves with the suffering brought about through *our own* condition.

235

I cannot fully separate myself from society, and I cannot fully integrate myself. I am nothing apart, and nothing wholly within. Individualism must lie in remaining a small part of a great mountain ... never disintegrating under pressure, but using that same pressure to become, like a diamond from a lump of coal, harder and brighter over time.

236

Society is the fast talking salesman, talks us into the corner and then charges rent for the whole of our existence. I am indebted for as long as I listen ... as long as I look beyond myself for rules.

237

Any device the institution uses to enslave I can use to master myself.

238

Look into the machinery of every lasting institution — especially those dedicated to a moral end: *their* power, manipulation, and indoctrination are not evil; only *my own* control of *my own* fate is evil. Very well then, I confess. I am the devil's closest ally, for this is the one thing I will never relinquish.

239

The question is not, "Where is society going?" ... but, "Where would 'I' go if I could take control ... *of myself?*"

Talking about control and *having* control are as different as giving
a sermon is from passing the collection plate around.

Upon great danger we abandon all laws and customs. It is by this
very mechanism that we abandon *determinism* to embrace a "first
cause," while in all other events we find security in our
mechanical world. Some use the "problems of Causation and
Logic" to make room for God and Free Will.

However, knowing that causality is dependent upon human
observation does not eliminate our dependence upon that
observation ... nor does the knowledge lessen the *usefulness* of
causality and logic to any degree. If we were carpenters building
a holy temple, would we throw away our hammers because they
were man-made?

In short, we reserve only for ourselves a "virtual freedom." We
know full well that we are inconsistent, just as we know full well
that our spirit is in danger of extinction. Life and happiness, if we
are ever to get them, are things we appropriate.

Which is the greater school for life, to enjoy privileges or to suffer
deprivation? I do not know the answer, but I do know this at least,
that I must learn from life as it presents itself. And in what other
way could I learn this than to grip *whatever* good or bad luck falls
into my hand. But in either pampering or adversity to ask —
"Why precisely *this?*" — is to drop the most valuable gem in
life: *our direct relationship with reality.* Real life begins only
after we shout boldly and firmly, "Even this!"

When some say we are not good conversationalists, what they
really mean is that we do not let them get a good enough grip

upon us. Reluctant wrestlers, we strip off and push away their "reaching out."

244

Truth is what it is to be human. If something is True, then it already belongs to us. Reserve the word "plagiarism" for those *non-human* facts we attribute to our natural selves ... just as we should reserve the word "scholar" for those who are ashamed of their own naked thought but somehow manage to stand before us confidently, wearing only their caps of authority.

245

Before, I could not stomach existence and had an appetite only for reading. Now I cannot keep a single word down. Books sit before me and I must talk myself into their value or my eyes will not move.

I consider this *real* progress.

246

1)   Arguments that are built upon names, dates and places are held by people wandering, as it were, through a labyrinth. There are conflicting signs, a historical "graffiti," strewn upon the walls, and it is their task to refute some of the signs and support some of the others, and through this method find their way from room to room. Of course, it goes without saying that for every passageway "correctly understood" there is an authoritative stamp which one might add to one's portfolio.

How do two such arguers proceed? At first we ourselves, as we listen and evaluate, are lost in the labyrinth of ideas, and so we cannot quite discern a method. However, if we were to conduct a small experiment and stop up our ears, while at the same time trusting only in our observations of *human behavior*, we would then discover their very simple method: the first task of two such arguers is to open their portfolios immediately and compare stamps.

2)   If, on the other hand, the arguers had no portfolios ... that is, if they followed a very strict method, forbidding all "name-dropping," appeals to external authorities, historical events ... in other words if the only "authorizations" permitted were those stamped by the actual experiences and confirmations of the arguers, then some confusion would first have to be overcome.

With the former method (1), the arguers believe that true progress is "proved" by an adequate number of authoritative stamps. These external authorizations — "proofs" — are held to be as relevant to the matter as personal confirmations are irrelevant. And passage from one set of "proofs" to another seems to be in accordance with the true order of nature. When they observe the latter (2), it could seem as if "progress" were not only impossible but life-threatening. "How can they possibly expect to find their way out of the labyrinth?"

The latter, himself, feels unfortunate and desperate ... as one would feel if thrown into deep water for the first time.

The former needs walls of names and dates and places upon a solid foundation if one is to have rooms through which one may receive the requisite stamps. For how else can he measure his "progress?" The latter also needs names and dates and places ... but so as to have actualities by which he might propel himself ... something from which he pushes *away*. In short, the former needs the walls in place, as proof of a progress no different from that of a traveler moving from point A to point B. The latter needs the external proof only in so far as it is that which he must necessarily leave behind ... that point from which he returns to *himself* ... to his own reality. He carries no "authorizations," for they would drag and sink ... would drown him. His personal state ... the *evolution* of that state is of no concern to the historian nor the nine-to-five philosopher — nor even to an acquaintance, for the very hint of such a progress would suggest a loss in rank for the stamp collector, and Ego rarely catches sight of the choice between *bad judgment* and *bruised ego* — the choice itself bruises. In short, true progress can only be *self*-confirmed.

The latter approaches genuine experience by paring away the not-me, assuming his own possession. The former, browbeaten, acts under the presumption that genuine experience belongs to someone else ... and that it is the task of life to wander, beg and borrow for that which he does not have ... that which he can never have. He finds nothing whatsoever in his own possession but a single resistance ... an objection to the method of the latter: "He does not even have a labyrinth, and so how can he expect to find a way out?"

247

The true benefit of our approach to a great mind is in our subsequent breaking away.

248

I must dust off this line between my sovereignty and my dependency every day. And I will not let others tell me to "be reasonable" with an encroachment, for it is always *their* encroachment that demands "reasonable behavior"; *my* encroachment always serves as an excuse for their retribution: conquest and the expulsion of my right to myself. Be reasonable? Let us recall the history of our borders. I met their external force with my force. They pressed all points of my sphere inward. I ceded much, but what I lost in size, I gained in *force* — until our opposing forces equalized. This point, where we both stopped, became our border. But be reasonable? I have won what little *force* I have by ceding much too much already. I won this ground and not by the laws of debate. I do not *claim it* by the laws of their institutions, but *have it* by the laws of nature. But be reasonable? I will not surrender an ounce of pressure by opening my mouth in further talk. This pressure is our agreement.

Amorality

249

Life itself prepares, but not all "preparations" encourage life. To see this clearly one must know that *what we must do* often opposes *what we should do* ... and if one is to have the scales tip *toward* life one must remove enough of the "shoulds" from the one side.

250

Our public "morality": The justifications for our inherited customs, which we defend tooth and nail for the sole reason that we have inherited them.

251

Moral behavior: Not only that which keeps a people together, but also the *justification* for their staying together.

Immoral behavior: Breaking rank, breaking away, becoming incomprehensibly simple ... unforgivably self-possessed.

252

Every inherited "morality" begins with an answer on whose behalf all questions must constantly rearrange themselves.

To be "immoral" is to *begin* with a question.

That which manages to *justify* our beginning with questions can only be "amoral." It is not "moral" in so far as it *begins* with the question. It is not "immoral" in that it has managed to *justify* such questioning. Even the *actualization* of honesty, they would have us believe, must be "amoral."

Public "Morals" and the Solitary Hunter: A true integrity respects the myriad offspring of existence ... both predator and prey. It never tries to reconcile two opposing, but necessary arguments. It maintains an ecological balance that will be destroyed if a species is allowed into an incompatible habitat ... for example, if our highest ambition were to stalk its prey within the meadow of our own "moral" approval. To tame the wilderness ... to make an organic process *"moral"* ... is to grope with a pale, hairless hand into the very depths of nausea. When will we understand our world? The lamb shall never lie with the lion ... although the lion may very well lie with some lamb.

Amorality: Concerned with testing and measuring the rules and standards of human behavior, as far as is humanly possible, beyond the interests of one's group and forever holding judgment between peace of mind and honesty ... not to mention all of the other conflicting interests dwelling within one's private laboratory ... "private," because it is the only laboratory possible.

Amorality is an attempt *not* to be "evil," just as much as it is an attempt to disregard the inherited "good" — yet better understood as the attempt *not* to be passive. Amorality is the attempt at a *real* self-control. It is the pursuit and application of those *mechanical forces* which account for human conduct.

Morality: "Concerned with accepted rules and standards of human behavior."

The word, "accepted," is where every *external morality* ends, for once we have proven the moral point *to ourselves* we have nothing more to do with its social "acceptability."

The only constancy with the external moral authority is its claim: "The rule is the same yesterday, today, and tomorrow."

With private human *becoming*, as I progress from stage to stage I also progress from "rule" to "rule."

The *method* of becoming has a constancy of its own, something which manifests itself as a "moral principle" ... or at least as a *physical* tendency toward the private recognitions of higher and higher "moral principles."

258

Strength is not in supporting blindly our public moral system. That is weakness. Strength is the *adjustment* of morality according to our private condition. However, what public morality has ever tolerated the adjustment of one of its own members without an involuntary defense: that of re-interpreting this as an "attack" and as originating from *outside* the bounds of the inherited morality? (Let us not forget that an externally imposed moral system will always appropriate the *"entire"* realm of morality to its own ends, which is usually nothing more than its own survival.) We in turn defend ourselves on *our* moral ground, which we regard as an attempt at moral legitimacy: our coldest observations of our nearest realities. We can not be *immoral* then, they say, for we lack passionate self-abandonment. No, we are worse than *immoral*, for we have no concern whatsoever for *their* morality.

259

Wherever I find "morality" and human behavior mutually exclusive, I exclude "morality." I hold my ground upon the *Real*: though I suffer, this is the *higher* suffering ... and though I might find relief or convenience in the "morality" of my culture, I cannot imagine any true joy in life that was not also a *human* joy.

The dilemma of the "wicked" experiment:

Do I follow it because it is "the path of least resistance?" That is, am I lazy? Or, do I avoid it from a fear of social denunciation and ridicule? That is, am I a coward?

There is a third, although rare, perspective: Will the experiment reveal what is or is not necessary to self-control and "mental" clarity?

However, with the removal of the word, "wicked," we have removed the public morality from consideration, and look only to a *Natural Law* which is no less real than the *Law of Gravity*. We no longer worry about the public tags, *"Laziness"* and *"Cowardice."* If leisure is necessary, well then so be it. If true courage can only be verified privately, well then so be it. *My morality* is not that morality which I have inherited from a random birth into an accidental culture: it is that morality which can only be acquired through a private struggle with reality. *My morality* consists of whatever is necessary to discover the laws of *human behavior* and to the establishment, thereby, of noble and self-affirming conduct. It is a personal, but nonetheless *empirical*, science ... with no appeal to tradition, authority, a "beyond," or *public* decency. Hence, if science is, to the public, "amoral," then it is no wonder that such experiments as mine are deemed "amoral" as well. I do not take its "amorality" as an objection ...

We consider science to be *amoral*. It does not act according to self-interest. It sees what it sees regardless of whether it is "Good" or "Evil." Its observations are grounded by solid reasoning and not distorted with human vanity, fear, or fancy. There is no place for the loss of pride when the scientist is in error, nor for the abundance of pride when his experiment is proven correct.

However, science is still a type of morality and can never be fully severed from the human tendency to apply the labels "good" and "bad." Consider: if empirical science precludes the "Ideal," it must then preclude "perfect objectivity" as well. In fact, the very rigidity of the scientific discipline implies our imperfection in this regard — not to mention our method of "trial and error." We are subject to sensory distortion, human drives, "paradigm shifts," cultural borders, etc. Next, consider that the scientist is still a *herd animal* ... a member of his own community, the members of which are more or less competent. Some manage to transcend their herd's presumptions better than others. Consequently, there is "Good" science and "Bad" science. Some scientists are condemned; others are praised. As scientists, we wish to "better" ourselves and so on. Thus, our community dependent science will always be a *moral* process. No matter what our assertions to the contrary, we blunder, and it is never long before *"Professional Ethics"* or *"Scientific Method"* becomes a backdoor through which the inherited morality makes its entrance in order to "save" or "correct" ... even "to interpret the data for the rest of us" — for our "scientific community" is at stake.

In all honesty and in respect for the term, "Morality," it is impossible for a human to be *amoral* — since to be human is to presume "Good" and "Evil" as a consequence of one's inheritance (yet hopefully with the simultaneous examination of that inheritance). Morality is a human reflex, and reflexes, by definition, are unavoidable. Changing the words "Good and Evil" into "right and wrong," "beneficial and harmful," "strong and weak," "scientific and unscientific," or whatever two opposites are chosen, is more of a repression of the moral phenomenon than it is an elucidation. Besides, such name-switching resembles, too keenly, the aforesaid attempts to "correct," "save," and "interpret" scientific findings.

We have worn the clothing of a superficial "morality" for so many millenniums that it is now a cause for shame to strip ourselves in public. The *natural* recognition has become a humiliating recognition. There is some irony here: for only when I value an "objective amorality," do I experience the humiliation. I do not rejoice in the loss of a false morality. Rather, I suffer from the loss of godly peers and feel my distance from the beasts closing ... yet I have already admitted to the impossibility of attaining the

82

"objective viewpoint"! Such a "perfect amorality," along with the foisted ideal, is a human delusion. On the other hand, my cultural presumptions, too, are delusions.

What remains in reality? What do I really want? When I value my own experience ... my own condition, when I appeal to nothing *beyond* myself ... why do I not rejoice at my personal communion with nature? Why prefer a glittering but false morality to a plain but true one? Human nature. We want our morality to "let us out of the prison of *the real*" ... and not to affirm *this* reality.

There can be no legitimate *good* without honesty, and in all honesty, we cannot reach farther than our own experience. A "true" morality, then, can only be a personal morality. Additionally, only *morality* is possible ... and this constitutes our problem insofar as we think of it as something either 1) External, like a debt passed down to us by our ancestors and toward which we must make our payments without question ... or as 2) Internal, something which we can actually *possess* ... something *more* than "objectively real" ... and certainly more than metaphysical.

A genuine Morality, even on this necessarily personal level, can not alter its nature on our account, for Morality is *our relationship with our own inexorable reality.* "I am here to be worked upon," as Emerson said. Objectivity is not a realistic objective, though it serves as a convenient reference point. As a metaphor, the North Star is not a destination. It, in itself, is not even a direction ... until the human first takes his own position as *the* point of reference. This was the beginning ... when the human eye then fixed the star to one spot in heaven and thereby charted his world. What *must* I take as my reference point? "I am a machine." Morality begins here ...

262

If the reader truly understands what I mean with the word "amorality," then the reader will understand that the choice of this word is of the least importance, while that which I attempt to represent is of the greatest. There is a problem with morality: that is, there are two claims to the throne. The usurper has crowned himself and laid down his self-serving laws, appropriating the title, "Morality." He is widely known by this name and has gained the approval of the entire realm, so that when the rightful claimant speaks of his private realm, and the laws pertaining to it, also under the name of "Morality," no one understands. They presume the definition as set by the usurper's culture, which they either defend or attack, and accordingly, they accept or reject all things "Moral."

We rightful claimants must find a new name — one which suggests our honest claim and direct descent from *sovereign nature* — one which suggests that our *private laws* are not built upon the same cornerstone as that of the *public laws* ... so that when we finish our castle no one is surprised that its form does not meet the public expectation. We claim *a personal and immediate relationship with nature ... natural laws governing a natural health.* They themselves, in their public perspective, think of this as a sort of "physician's prescription" — "scientific" — *"Amoral."* We do not quibble, for we love nature's own morality, and care nothing for the titles under which we are to rule ... so long as we rule.

263

My "Good" is a progression from lower states of clarity toward higher states. I do not chain myself to any particular "understanding" but to the *physiological progression* itself. Any given "understanding" will soon be discarded in favor of the next, higher interpretation. What one is *holding on to,* by way of a few iron habits, can also be called the *right* to the future. The entire process demands greater and greater acquisitions of self-control. This self-control turns upon itself the aim of greater clarity ... and again, for the sake of finding the way to even more control.

Now, if *you*, dear reader, also seek the same progression, then *you* understand me, for you *live* me. And your understanding me is only confirmation that you have previously understood *yourself.* And this constitutes the interdependence of *our* immortality. Each of us must first draw our own line, scratching *out* the boundary

84

claimed by our own external authorities (from whom we never receive "permission" to do so) and, without moving so much as a hair's breadth, we *find* ourselves already within *this* self-appropriated center ... *within* the *genuine experience,* the explanation of which forces a contradiction: *You and I* <u>*share the uniqueness*</u> *of what it is to exist ... you and I, and others like us, will experience each other ... come alive and recognize each other. We pass along this genuine experience like a flame, from torch to torch — and here and there, looking down upon the vast expanse of darkness, find a flicker or two lighting up the way.*

264

When the word "Expediency" becomes redundant, superfluous and irrelevant — when it remains as vestige ... as evidence of a previous misunderstanding of reality, it will also serve as proof that the word "Morality" no longer designates "tractability" nor "stupidity" ... but has gained a legitimacy and cause for our genuine respect.

As it is now, however, to "fight" for the sake of "morality" is to suffer oneself to be hit on the head with a rubber mallet. One's own dedication to dignity ... one's own suit and tie, only *heighten* the impulse for laughter. Better to pay respects to expediency ... to step aside and let the clown trip over its own oversized shoes.

If the word, "Good," has indeed distanced itself from reality, it has become a joke, and we cannot deny the world its punch line without also denying its cause for joy and laughter. This moral clown *must* fall. When it pretends that it cannot fall ... when it pretends to height and dignity ... when precisely our distance from reality is called, "morality" ... it is then only a matter of seconds before the comic fall ... before our involuntary laughter, whose meaning we fail to grasp. The tower of comedy would not be *comedy* if it did not fall. Recognizing *Morality* is no different. It is our descent to reality ... a cause for joy and laughter.

What the public morality calls "amoral" is nothing more than the *highest* morality possible ... never mind that it is the *only* morality possible. What the public calls "moral" is only "wishful thinking" or a means to harness the masses.

It is only when the individual severs from the group, becomes a whole unto himself ... when he takes responsibility for his own life and accepts the bounds of his *own* reality ... it is only at this point that he becomes *moral.*

Repetition: The Redemption of the Ideal

The brain is the fulcrum upon which a trinket lifts the infinite.

There must be, of course, only one ultimate reality. (I am speaking of a physical and not "metaphysical ultimate reality.") However, the human brain is not equipped to perceive that single reality. Instead we have multiple and therefore fragmented perceptions upon the single ultimate reality ... perceptions from which we then reconstruct, on our own terms, a "mental whole." This "mental whole" is not the same as the *physical* "ultimate" reality. However, the evolution of the "mental whole" is more than just a series of errors: it serves as a kind of "sign posting" .... a finding one's way toward higher and higher perceptions. *This mental whole*, this reconstruction of the universe through the resolution of contradictions, is my "spiritual" process and is dependent upon a *natural phenomenon* which I like to call, "Repetition."

The Manifestations of Reality:

A. As incomprehensible immediate sensory impressions.

B. As impressions held in the memory in two important forms and thereby rendered comprehensible and useful:

    1. As an instance, a fact isolated from a whole.

    • As involuntary snapshots of reality.

- As scientific method: facts subjected to empirical confirmation and sound reasoning, creating a sort of periscope from which we might see around the limitations of our senses. Thus, we see beyond "common sense," learning that it is the Earth which revolves around the Sun and not the reverse.

2. As a type, a repetition of instances forming a single, cerebral impression, isolated from a whole.

- With the instances forgotten through a process called repetition-blindness, the events manifest themselves cerebrally as "Reasons," "Ideals," "Laws," "a priori," "Causation," "Truth," "Universal," etc.

- Such repetitions, when flayed by the "surface" view — that is, when restricted to "fact" and "formula" can only be seen as "Myths" ... and here the "existential vacuum" begins.

- Self-behaviorism, as organic method: preferred repetitions contributing to higher and more accurate recognitions of *"Truth."*

269

For my *not* having been born Emperor, I have been fortunate. I simmered ... I plotted ... I changed the rules and object of the game ... and in the end found compensation in my rise to a very *real* sovereignty. My cunning had stumbled upon the only thing which could remain pure without being at the same time smug.

But all those around me see only a crown without jewels and studded with only the "smallest" concerns: fish for breakfast, "cerebral hygiene," and a handful of petty habits. They laugh and propose my "coronation," not rejecting a higher nobility as much as showing disgust for reality. Their reality, it seems, is beneath them.

270

There is a man I know who thinks that an earthquake in Chile which killed 30,000 people is more calamitous than the handful of petty habits which will kill him before the year is up.

271

I just turn the key and the tiger in me leaps out, does whatever damage it pleases, and then trots back to its cage with that majestic presumption that I will feed it again for tomorrow's romp. And I do ... because I am nothing without this key.

272

I suspect that my ideas will grow together, not so much as evidence that the universe is ordered, but that *the brain* tends to organize chaos into a single, orderly perspective. It would roll up my many jewels into a single velvet cloth ... as the evidence and redemption of my experience.

273

Is repetition *real*? Or is it only memory which makes repetition appear real ... the eyes which are truthful, and which, under a strict and immediate scrutiny, never find a repetition.

... or on the contrary, is there some other region of the brain which makes *the particular* appear real, memory performing greater judgment than the eyes? ... every particular, in some minute aspect, deviant and foreign to the repetition.

Yet these mutually exclusive aspects of reality belong to a universe which can only be *one*. That we cannot fathom the inconsistency can only be explained by admitting to a limitation of the human mind.

Reality is *one thing*. It is the mind that *must* split, contrast, see the particular at one moment and then the repetition in the next ... for it craves the material from which it might *re*-construct that *one thing*.

Forgive the contradictions: An actuality provokes an immediate response, and we are confident in our reality. A tendency, however, is not an immediate actuality, and therefore, under this strict definition, not a reality at all. It is a succession of actualities which endure as impressions upon another immediate actuality: the brain. It is a cerebral event, requiring the grouping of selected impressions into one place and time. We see the *conclusion* of a series, and often mistake it for or place it within the left-hand side of an equation of actualities.

The captain who tacked east and west against the north wind could never be seen in his northward bent ... but at last he struck the ice. Now suppose that this collision cracked open the side of the ship and a prisoner held within the dark hull for the entire journey stepped out upon the ice, held up his fists to the sky and rejoiced. This cerebral actuality, this beginning, this single point has no historical accounting with which to recognize a *tendency* but is an immediate experience and belongs to the left side of the equation — to the side of immediate actuality. It is not a *destination* but will soon become a *point of departure* for the memory.

In the end, without cerebral function, all is a single reality and belongs neither on the left side nor the right side of the equation. What accounts for the existence of the "left side of our equation"? A sensory organ which snips immediate impressions off of a whole reality. What *should* find itself on the right side? A cerebral organ which recognizes the repetitions of these *same* impressions. What do we have instead on this right side? Human vanity ... an "Ideal" foisted back onto reality ... a falsehood constructed out of our limited view so that we might imagine a *safe* whole.

I cannot sustain my argument for long, for I have already shown that *there is no equation:* the human species has made a problem of existence, and this manufacturing of the "equation" is a problem in itself, but it is a problem for behaviorists, not philosophers. Subjectively, the destination of my journey is real, even as a *tendency*. Objectively, however, it is only as real as it is *immediate*. I look through the lens of this cerebral device and can see nothing but this dual image of my world. Nature has turned the lens until the immediate actuality becomes a *projected* repetition, and yet it is precisely this *projected* repetition which interprets all immediate impressions. In a reality of surfaces, I find depth — but where formerly it was the "depth" of *left-side* infiltration and infinite extensions of the equation, now it is the *depth* of mistrust in all "human equations" that do not admit to themselves as *behavioral phenomena*.

275

The universal and the particular are two different manifestations of one reality. That is all. It is the human experience that makes a duality of nature. It could be said that 1. Plato's Ideal, 2. the cerebral consequence of repetition, and 3. the particular are *three* separate manifestations ... if it were not that Plato's Ideal is merely an appropriation of the natural phenomenon of repetition ... his *natural error* (and every human's illusion) being that this manifestation exists independent of the human experience, preceding it — whereas repetition has in the meanwhile played upon the senses, worked in the memory, become *one thing* to the memory.

276

The *complete* realist sees from an "ideal" vantage point. The idealist, of course, does the same. The only difference: the realist recognizes that he brings repeated instances into the present moment by way of a single, integrated recollection — whereas the idealist will not *recognize* that he does the same. And why not? ... because the *other world*, the *predominance of mind*, and even *order itself* seem to be at stake.

Once upon a time, when *Instance* made love to *Repetition* ... unto the great Cerebral, the one and only *God,* two children were born, with equally convenient names, *Fact* and *Ideal.* Now Fact took after Instance, and Ideal was the spitting image of Repetition. Both grew with a perfect equanimity:

"It's all yours," said the *Fact* to the *Ideal.*

"And yours too," said the Ideal to the Fact.

"After you," invited the Ideal.

"No, after you ... I insist."

Now our God, like we mortals, had two organs for perception and was pleased at the sight. In one eye He was nearsighted, seeing only Fact. In the other, He was farsighted, seeing only the Ideal. And so it was that from this perfect distance and direct point of view, He could see in perfect harmony, Fact and Ideal, as they frolicked side by side in clear view.

I must tell the reader that it was out of love and not mistrust that He drew nearer to embrace His children. God was completely innocent, for upon arrival, only Fact had remained, only the immediate was embraced. The Ideal, so it seemed, had refused His love, but this was only because God was completely blind to the Ideal at this distance. For in His approach, in His eagerness to touch, only the exception to the rule stood out, only Fact remained palpable. The Fact and only the Fact could be verified. And more importantly, the Fact alone could be embraced by the *a priori* ... could be connected by the "inherent" *geometry* of the mind.

So it was that God was frustrated by His unrequited love for the Ideal. In bitterness, He cast himself down from heaven and dwelt among all of the other beasts of the Earth, and out of his strict and sincere honesty, made a solemn vow to crush all his precious "idols" ... all his most cherished "falsehoods." This destruction, however, presented him with a problem, for the Ideal, "not existing in reality," could not be grasped, let alone struck. As the reader would guess, it was not long before this cleverest of all the beasts had the solution: in short, his bad eye was the offense and so he must pluck it out. And he did so in a rather brilliant manner: he walked around, set his vantage point askew of the duality ... aligned himself in such a way that the unverifiable Ideal — the idol of the mind — vanished from view ... eclipsed by Fact.

Needless to say, our demoted god was compensated for the loss of his Ideals, for the corollary to the loss of Error can only be the acquisition of Truth. *Real* truth! He, as mortal, was pleased and congratulated himself on this perfect and necessary "refutation." He fixed himself to this vantage point, while his one and only visible child, Fact, marched lockstep down the path, premise after premise, conclusion after conclusion, gaining distance from the fixed vantage point and adding up to ... accumulating into ... and it was just then, from his fixed vantage upon the real, that he could begin to see, step by step, the Fact *repeating* itself. In the next instant, a sliver of the Ideal pealed off from behind the Fact! The Ideal emerged just as when the crescent sun moves out and enlarges itself from behind the dark moon! Our error, *returned!* and with a vengeance, forming a new whole and perfect repetition! Fathering that ... that *mistake* ... "Dear me!" The mortal shouted in a state of rational panic, "It looks like ... it appears ... This will ruin all! *It* is only an appearance — I am sure of that — but this new and more perfect Ideal is beginning to look like ... my Geometry ... my *a priori!* Away! Away with all geometry! Move! Askew! The world is absurd! It can only be seen *Askew!*"

The Human Process

278

Perhaps with this approach (philosophy as behavior) there is tremendous room for error ... but I am also saying that there is *certain* error with the absolute obedience to a system of logical rules. A looser, "amoral" observation and self-application has a better chance.

There are no magic words, just as there are no instant values. The confusion arises when we think we are scientists etching a complex formula on a chalkboard, when in reality we should be simple farmers weeding and cultivating a garden of preferred habits and stimuli.

280

The habit-path: The difference between our species and a water-shrew is that we can "classify" experience and apply an old lesson to a completely new environment. The water-shrew, as the ultimate realist, is too perfect ... too "honest" to continue an old presumption into the new circumstance ... not for very long anyway. When something new is brought into its environment, it does not play false to the immediate world. It very quickly comes upon the difference and begins its correction. It tries out *new paths* through the *new environment* over and over again in order to perfect the new, highly efficient habit-path. In short, the water-shrew is the perfect scientist; its presumptions are soon encountered, and immediate sense perception takes over and corrects all previously learned lessons.

Our great advantage, on the other hand, is our "dishonesty" to the immediate world ... our *unrealism* ... our ability to say, "This is like that" or "This is not like that." We take two contrasting experiences and, through a *greater capacity* for recognizing repetition, find them summed up into a third cerebral experience and call what would be *immediately* false the "Truth" ... and it is the truth.

But Truth recognition is also our great disadvantage. Our environment changes, but we do not. A rock introduced and the water-shrew collides, stops, then relearns. Darwin writes a book, and the human collides, stops ... and collides again, and again, for one or two hundred years.

Should I defend *myself* or defend the *Truth*? I am the captain with one foot in each of two boats and it is my chief task to persuade, convince, threaten, cajole my separate crews to remain coordinated ... keep the course true so that I am not forced into one boat at the expense of the other. *

* "But the truth never strays!"

"Which truth? There are *'truths'* that take you away from yourself just as there are *'truths'* that bring you back."

282

My growth depends upon the life cycle of truth: the birth of wonder, its maturing into a certainty, its infection with doubt and suspicion, and then it's sudden death as a lie.

283

For every lie I kill, I find another innocent truth grazing in the meadow.

284

I am not constructing a system for truth, but discovering the stippled image of my task and training my reflexes to serve this task. And it often seems to me that this newly revealed task is nothing other than to add another dab of paint to the image ... a task for the task, if you will.

285

Why this fear that we will somehow lose the human spirit? Have we not admitted that we can never see around ourselves? ... that despite all our efforts we are still just as attached as before? No, the human flame is brighter than our objectivity is dark. It may gutter under the breath of our coldest arguments, yet every word which fails to snuff us out inflames us.

286

I am the universal system, but the stuff of which it is made, my certainties, will not have it so. Predator and prey, at times *I* stalk the infinite ... for that brief moment until it swallows me whole again.

287

Man is organic. He only need remain rooted in the soil where he finds himself. He *grows* his meaning. Like the Amazon, he estimates more species than he can hope to name.

288

A human is an expanding equation. We tend to think a lot of ourselves, and so this equation usually totals up to more than what we actually are. However, in the aftermath of a great disaster, the error is usually discovered. We reduce and simplify the equation, in human fashion, *to the extreme.* Our equation is then *less* than our actuality ... which is also to say that our *actuality* is then *more* than our *equation.* Existing now, well beyond our own definitions, we become the objects of our own wonder, so how could we then settle for such a small, inadequate equation of ourselves? The equation expands.

The Door of Ennui

289

Why human progress has been slow: Though we crave power, we have no instinct for its acquisition and very little respect for the actual mechanics of force. We have very little defense against an immediate response to a present stimulus and then, even if we were able to withstand this immediate trial, we would still remain intoxicated by our past conditioning. More often than not, we settle only for the trappings of power — would sooner hold a scepter than work the lever.

The necessary task, then, is to realize that we search for power in darkness and can only discover its general direction, with all the accompanying excitement of a mathematical equation.

290

"Declare war and leave victory as the only way out" — proof that one's eyes have not yet opened. One is *always* at war ... has always been at war. We are not only *bored*, we are blind.

291

Repetition is the only thing one can grip; the surface, the only thing one can let go. Yet we fly from repetition as though from a boring neighbor ... running for those spectacular celebrities who ignore our existence before they suddenly leave us.

292

We have finally discovered that the word "freedom" has floated away from the center, and in its place we find the word, "Boredom." Boredom is a satiety which nevertheless *still lacks something* ... a want of excitement, by which we preserve an advantage: deadened *needs* permit us to introduce stimuli with delicate, retractable instruments.

Ennui! ... but how to endure the unendurable?! ... how to keep our hands from trembling with excitement before its promises?! ... for only in boredom do we find ourselves *above* our needs, searching for *something higher* than cheap stimuli ... only in this state can we *test* excitements ... dig new channels so that one's desires flood on toward a higher, newly *constructed* need. *We rise and one day spill over into a new satiety!*

Energy and Mechanical Force

293

As far as living my life is concerned, the discovery of mechanical force has been the only Truth worth my efforts.

294

What could be more useless than to comprehend the secret of the universe? A man would almost think that he could then do away with dinner.

295

I can handle more than my mind can grasp.

296

Whatever falls from the highest state of excitement has a ring of authenticity that cannot be muffled out, not even by the intention behind the utterance.

297

"Will Power" is a *constructed response* ... a bracing ourselves against a natural response which we perceive *as harmful.* However, more effective than such "Will Power" is the substitution of one stimulus for another. And where one cannot substitute, one can at least disperse the power of a harmful stimulus by introducing competitive stimuli.

Taste is a stimulant; nutrition is essential — unequal in the power of appeal — but also unequal in the effect, and that should be enough to tip the scales. But it does not. The former remains as appealing as the latter remains effective. Perhaps we can enlarge this into a metaphor for the entire human problem: our *ideas of life* are as stimulating as the *mechanics of life* are essential.

Ultimately, we must have *faith* that mechanical forces govern our lives completely. We cannot know all, but must have a nose for the way. To deny past tendencies, the overall direction of past discoveries ... to face our destination but walk backwards ... that was the consequence of our previous *faith*.

Of one war, how insane are the instigators if it is a civil war; if it is a war of independence, how noble. To the victor belong the spoils ... which includes all of the meaning and justification in an enterprise.

The finger on reality, the mind on ideas: An infected finger can alter the movements of the whole body, while a bad idea can stop the body altogether ... but that is not to say that a better idea can then set the whole body into motion again ... there, the finger has us again.

Freedom and Force

The struggle *for* freedom and the struggle *after* freedom is won are so dissimilar as to make a man feel he was mistaken to seek freedom in the first place. When faced with *"What was it that I really wanted?"* he can no longer explain his frustration, except to say that now he does not seem to have needed so much ... only this next thing that seems to be withheld from him.

302

If I waddle somewhat toward where I need to go, my desires and whims *follow* like a brood of ducklings. If I stop to gather them in, they scatter ... and *I* chase after.

303

Too often "freedom" is another word for "ignorance." It serves as a palliative for our shock at seeing the gears and levers behind our nature.

304

One finds a method for happiness and saddens all others by trying to convert them to the same. Perhaps happiness is in the *finding* ... just as sadness would lie in not having permission to search.

305

The most beneficial events in my life have involved the *loss* of freedom.

306

He who does not want control but wants to live is doomed.

307

Freedom is not the absence of limitations; freedom is using limitations to one's own advantage.

308

Mediocrity is unrestricted force.

Freedom: Our species seeks the absence of limits ... craves to feel itself *free* of all constraint. Of the grain of sand, it would see infinity ... of this passing moment, eternity. Somehow we are to blink away the wall of reality.

However, suppose one sought freedom in the opposite direction, groped hand over hand along the wall, *so as to be sure of its inexorability* ... to have something *unyielding* to push off from.

One cannot push off from *unlimited* freedom. Freedom as I have experienced it requires a limit. Seeing this limit requires courage. This limit renders control. And however deficient it may be, this limit ... *this control* is something like freedom.

There is no reasonable assurance that, within the limited influence of a mere book, a writer could turn a reader around and send that reader in any particular direction. An apple must be ripe and heavy or the breeze of ideas will not release it to the law of gravity.

If we had *complete* control of every aspect of others' lives, for perhaps at least three generations, maybe it could be done ... but we would not need a book. All fruit would ripen and fall at the right time, the only problem being that the world regards *any* attempt at real control as a *loss* of freedom.

What we would never believe: Picking the lock is an admission that one has been chained. One feels humiliated. Consequently, one denies the existence of one's chains.

What we often believe: Dealing with Stimulus and Response is an admission that one is not as free as one would like to believe. One feels humiliated. Ironically, this humiliation itself serves as a stimulus whose response is to deny the entire role of Stimulus and Response.

"Free will" does not exist, at least not in the manner we speak of it. It is an error, just as "mind" is an error. What happens? The clamor above the surface of things enters the labyrinth of the ear and returns again as an echo ... a harmonized chorus. Throughout our music there are pleasant and seductive melodies that flatter us. One of them is "free will."

We hardly notice the cadence punctuating our melody ... and to which our muscles are dancing. If there is such a thing as control, it is here in the cadence and tempo of our thoughts and not their melody and lyric. I dare not call this "will" ... for fear that I will be seduced out of my rhythm again.

Let me stop the music here, as I often must, and scold the members of my orchestra: "You are not inside me; you are outside me: I face you. I select you, arrange you, fashion for you your instruments. It is only in this manner that I can *compose* something beautiful *from within*. Now lay this next melody over the beat of my heart ... are you ready?"

314

313

Thus, my task and method: To seduce the *body* to the rhythm of the music around me ... *by composing that music* ... which in turn can only be done by the arrangement of all of my players.

The Stimulus and the Self

314

The function of a stimulus is not to help one *get by*, nor to endure, but to forget the human condition altogether. To decrease the number and frequency of key stimuli, therefore, is to explore the depths of one's humanity ... a first experience that feels more like remembering ... but how many confuse this with boredom?

315

We like to say that we generalize an event in order to have a maxim for all occasions ... but we, the creators, know that we are also concealing its petty origin.

316

I can already smell the rot of his argument. I have no other refutation than this: its truthfulness repels me. That there is a dunghill on my left may be true, but it is equally true that there is a green meadow on my right.

317

The aim of truth is not to *convince*, nor is it to *define*, but to turn the listener's eyes toward that which the speaker sees. We speak, however specific the words, only in a general direction. There is still much in truth which the listener must *guess*.

318

For significance and comprehension, the stimulus of the written word is at least as important as its validity.

319

Dreams, Spirit, Soul, Religion, Philosophy ... all "other worlds" make no difference at all, which is to say that they can be believed, *harmlessly* ... as long as all necessary *things* are in place.

320

A phrase has meaning only so long as it points to me ... either to greater power or pleasure, loss or pain ... but let that finger fall from my own chest and it points down to the abyss opening beneath my feet.

The question is not just *where does the word place the reader?* ... but also *where is it sending him?* Teach a child mathematics in the classroom. Take the same child to the toy store, give him a budget, and teach the child how to answer his own questions. Or, on the other hand, show the child how much money he cannot have and what he cannot therefore buy. Then show the child what he could have purchased and teach the child how to answer his own questions. In short, that which points toward or away from self-empowerment has significance.

322

The appeal of truth is mysterious because it is the total repetition — and not the instance — of stimulus-response. We see the instance before us, as if it were a white wall, and we read and write much more "into it" than can possibly be justified. This *conditioning*, ignored, accounts for a large part of what humans call "depth." Now, that we consider this fact "depressing" signals another aspect of human perception: we do not really want depth so much as we want to escape from superficiality. Had we really wanted *depth*, we would have embraced repetition as the means toward greater and more significant experiences. We prisoners of the heart! At last we have the key in our hand — but do not know which side of the door is *out* and which is *in*.

323

The argument is not stimulating enough; consequently, it is invalid. Also, arguments *grow* invalid as I distance myself from a key stimulus.

Now that I am aware of the growth and decay involved in human reasoning, my task is to grow a new, *grand* argument, an accretion of disparate but necessary relationships with *things*, where all of these disparate truths, through cultivation, *grow* towards each other and eventually join, not logically, but nonetheless *necessarily.* The unifying principle? The germ of a grand argument? ... the repetition of *key stimuli.*

324

A truth may not mention repetition, but it is always dependent upon it. Truth is the manifestation of repetition.

325

An admired thinker becomes something like a favorite comedian: everything the comedian does, even walking on stage with a serious face, provokes laughter ... as with the thinker, everything petty finds its way toward significance.

326

We are meaningless within the realm of reason and surface, but not within that of sensation. And within the realm of sensation there are two types: that which passes and that which endures. The former is the instance provoking a sensation. It is both the promise of meaning and the breaking of that promise. The latter is the sensation of repetition itself. It alone has the power to keep promises.

Desire Versus Necessity

327

My last hope: Patience is not a virtue. It is a consolation. What a man extends too far nature lops off, and he calls this surviving half, *patience.* Let us not give false honor to this maimed virtue. Patience, harnessed to the necessary, is no longer "patience," but the goddess herself, *nature.* Give me that harness, shield my eyes from all that requires hope, and I will sing my way up the mountain, as high as the goddess will take me ... with never a *need* to console myself in the knowledge that I cannot climb higher.

328

My Life Strategy: The management of immediate stimuli for the sake of a necessarily slow, *accumulative* indulgence in the approach toward a grand end.

329

Happiness may be an obstacle to true fulfillment. We are too comfortable to *feel* what is necessary to the task.

330

He fancies he can bend fate and not break it, but nature has not bent a hair's breadth ... has not repealed one jot nor tittle of its laws and snaps the creature in two.

331

Only necessity is certain ... and at the expense of all else. Desire, for or against necessity, accounts for all of the happiness and misery in the world.

332

There will always be servants and masters, because society *needs* them. Perhaps it even needs the glutton and the emaciated, as points of measurement — as one cannot know the center of a circle without knowing the perimeter.

It would follow then that a society that produced only moderate citizens would never know its true center of necessity. It would then in all probability be unable to remain moderate. Being unable to distinguish between necessity and desire, it would see only its desires, until it approached the perimeter of necessity ... to put it in other words, until threatened with extinction ... that is, if it be so fortunate as to be threatened beforehand.

333

All that is worthy and pure in life is born out of the wedlock of desire and necessity, but there are too few honorable matchmakers for the betrothal, for it is within human nature to ravish the desire and estrange it from the necessary. The marriage becomes, from the beginning, an awkward arrangement.

334

A wise man is one who sees, however obscurely, *through* his desires and upon what is necessary to cultivate those desires. The average man, on the other hand, is blinded to the necessary by the very clarity with which he sees his desires.

335

I pour this tea. I want the tea, and so I tilt the pot up a little further. The tea, however, pours through the spout just as fast as before ... with the exception that now much of it spills through the lid. I have saved no time, have satisfied myself no sooner, and have made a mess of the whole matter. What have I learned? That an effort should be made to pull back my desires to the borders of necessity ... *but no further:* I do not want to *root out* my desires, but *satisfy* them. This is what others call *"moderation,"* but we know it to be the extreme, since there is no faster, more efficient way. The human tragedy, then, would be to desire the extreme, but to have no eyes for it.

336

Why formulate hypothetical solutions to hypothetical problems when there are *real* problems at hand? ... the first problem being our desire to flee from the *necessary* by burying our heads in the hypothetical.

The important thing is to sink my nails deep into the necessary, for it is not the necessary itself but the tenacity of my grip upon it that deepens me. In a word, repetition. Only repetition bores deeply into the surface of things. *What* repeats is of secondary importance.

One task in life is to learn that one must graduate from the lower rank of problems to the higher. The next task is to learn that this is done *by gripping the necessary.* The lowest of our species, however, circle round the base of their task, mumbling their clever little riddles and chasing the skirts of petty stimuli without seeing that necessities spiral *upward and inward ... but only as our grip upon them is unrelenting.*

If one cannot refine desire, which destroys everything — *fast,* then one will never yield to necessity, which builds all things, but *slow.*

Habits and Construction

We do not have beliefs or arguments; we have customs. Take away a man's belief and he refutes the theft. Take away a custom and he drowns in despair.

My goals: First, to recall the exiled half of myself, the amoral human. Second, to allow all opposing forces to fix me in place, just as an axle remains fixed by the opposition of spokes: this bit of good here, this bit of evil there, here a friend, there an enemy, here an inconsistency that I neither deny nor resolve. And third, to roll on this wheel of habits ... roll on the power of my own nature.

342

I define error as a disadvantageous *reflex*. I reduce all mistakes to poor training.

343

Setting a new habit: One cannot lift a cogwheel into the air, let go, and expect it to remain, and so we must find one or two other wheels which are already in place and then position the new wheel accordingly. The morning or evening rituals are the best places to begin. One then approaches the chaos of midday, piecemeal, slowly assembling a productive machine from the strewn and wasted parts of an uncultivated life.

344

There is a breaking point when setting a habit, much like the violent collapse of sound in a sonic explosion. In the tremendous silence and smooth gliding afterward, one no longer comprehends the difficulties.

345

Turbulence: All significant change is violent and lies precisely with those customs whose immutability my peers have already taken for granted. The river is white. I can not swim in turbulence. I let it carry me, wait for calmer waters ... hope for the best.

The Calm: I do not need symbols or metaphors ... anymore than I need thoughts or spirits. I set these aside for story telling. What I need is great health, stimuli toward life, an ascending network of habits, objects strategically placed, and most of all, courage and stamina to grip a new repetition, grip all *necessary* change until that higher law, *stability,* conquers all.

Imagine the awareness of "mind" as something similar to standing at the edge of a pond, all of the autumn colors ... all of the creatures in our life shimmering in reflection upon it ... and where much of the luster of the reflection depends upon the purity of the water. Now imagine that this reflection is our *only* view of this small world. Would we not do everything we could to preserve the purity of the water? ... blindly, as best we can, work the landscape, turn the woods into aviaries, tame the deer, kill only the closest snakes, let all distant predators run wild? And would we not look back at ourselves and laugh at our former attempts at "self-improvement" ... *by plunging our hands into the water?*

It is an error to believe that all must be in order before one "begins." The truth is that nothing organizes chaos like the ongoing process, habit ... and so, all has already been locked to its order *before one "begins."*

A *true* "beginning" would be just another word for "chaos" and if any true organization took place at the "beginning" then it would only be because we associate the word "beginning" with another meaning: one has already acquired experience and knows what to do, and so what is called here a "preparation" or a "beginning" is really a continuation ... an ongoing repetition whose course and destination one already knows how to alter. The process itself has no beginning or middle or end. And it is not chaos, but order itself, the *momentum* of custom, that stands in the way of a great "beginning." This momentum is too great for us to resist *en masse.* We press against this great ship to whose course we are bound, but we do not move so much as an inch. We must recruit and train, one by one, a thousand hands and then only by exerting ourselves, tirelessly, with small thrusts again and again can we "begin." That is to say, only by cajoling, forcing, retraining, resisting, substituting, and eliminating the most petty habits, *one by one,* will we have the thousand hands necessary to alter our course, albeit ever so slowly. This *"change in course"* is the only real "beginning" possible. And it is indeed poignant to observe those who forever "wait for a chance to begin," for "waiting" itself has its momentum.

349

The world is round, but I spend my life searching for a corner.

350

If I spin with my universe, it could be said that I do not spin at all ... as an illusion or as a reality.

351

My heart beats. I breathe. Are these *movements?* The sun rises every morning and I arise. Are these *movements?*

It is not "I" who makes these "movements."

352

I am not trying to overtake my own time. In fact, I am trying very hard not to move at all.

353

Life is not made up of problems that we *think through,* but of relationships towards things: customs. To put it another way, life is something that we *cultivate* ... something that *yields fruit* ... and with cultivation, quantity of days at minimal effort is more fruitful than the maximal effort of a single day. Only that which increases has value, and only that which can be sustained, increases.

All growth requires a trusting passivity, just as a seed requires certain elements of nature — sunlight and water, but mostly, time spent in one place, in the undisturbed, fertile soil ... in a germinating stillness. The only movement one needs is that which keeps the elements in place.

354

My Repetition: To strengthen my grip upon myself ... *to remain on the anvil*, mute and passive ... to turn everything soft *into* the falling hammer and to love the pounding ... to find joy in this natural instinct to grow stronger ... for the first time to feel, not the tremors of fear, but the vibrations of the *whole*.

355

The human is a mirror of his reality. Reality is not static. How can we then set up, as a goal, a "static self"? The world is in *flux*. Awareness joins that *flux* by gripping its debris. Only by participating in real change does one affirm reality.

356

We grow in increments but manifest ourselves in the moment of comparison. Great events measure the fact; they do not nurture it. The blunder in life is to mistake this *measuring* for the growth itself. To say it in another way, grand events manifest the accumulation of all our smallest moments more than they add to our totality. Who we are does not make us; that which makes us does not reveal our growth ... but like clouds which gather energy silently and invisibly, and in an instant, bond, flash and split the tree ... but who cares for the history of that force as much as its demonstration?

Even "chaos" travels in circles. Ironically, it is usually the "lack of a routine" that *returns* one back to the point of origin. The "traveler" soon despairs. He blames *repetition* and cannot reconcile himself to it in any form. To break the monotony, he flies after the nearest bright stimuli, again and again, and rarely sees that he travels in a circular trail *of avoidance*. Life becomes, not a momentum toward new adventures, but a series of stultifications, a protracted friction unto the inevitable collapse of the spirit ... followed by a tremendous, enervating expenditure, if one is to begin everything ... *again!* To start and stop ... as a repetition ... what else could be hell? But how to see this prison, repetition, *as the freedom*?

We can train ourselves for a sudden and inevitable great empowerment with small, regular doses of pain ... *to the point of pleasure*. The pain of setting an exercise routine for example ... of tearing muscles or straining the heart daily.

Perhaps this is anticlimactic to the promise of an aphorism, but with the framework of Christianity still in place, I feel it necessary to let the reader know I am not speaking of hair shirts, but of the natural reflex *against* replacing one habit for another ... no matter how advantageous this new habit may be ... and that every advance toward distant, accumulated pleasures and values demands just this sharp, immediate pain of tearing and rebuilding ... *as a daily, petty affair*.

Acceptance lies in habituating the unpleasant. To accept my unconditional death, for example, I only need to affirm my condition for a sufficient length of time. As with all things, the unpleasantness of disillusionment lessens with *repetition*. I then proceed to affirm my life ... to steer it from a stark authenticity to a cycle of increasing value.

A: Is it more pleasurable without the obstacle?

B: Yes, but before I discovered that it was an obstacle, I was content. There was no inconvenience, and therefore, there was no obstacle.

A: But if it is "better" without the obstacle, would it not be wise to look for other comfortable, and therefore *invisible* obstacles everywhere?

Unless I see the mind as the backward thinking creature ... unless I see "will" as a looking into a mirror ... as merely a conditioned response to stimuli and therefore *inverted* and *late* ... then I am less free than foolish.

Where "mind" has not yet trained the muscles and nerves, fed the stomach, rearranged the surface, discriminated between stimuli, has not rewritten the history of the man ... where mind is not yet machine, but "soul" ... "operating" somewhere "beyond" the material world ... where all immediate stimuli and past conditioning are scratched out of the equation of an *act* ... in short, where 'will' thinks of itself as captain, there I will find only a deluded stowaway who, upon seeing a reef just ahead, leaps up from below deck and commands the *ship* to turn away ... *by pointing his finger.* Never mind the current of the sea, the inertia of the vessel, never mind the wind, the rudder, the sails, never mind the undisciplined crew, never mind my low rank ... it seems enough to point the finger.

"Will," if it even exists at all, is the weakest of the influences upon a man's destiny; consequently, it must become the most cunning, flattering, knowledgeable stowaway a ship has ever held below deck ... but then one does not ... *can not* realize this until *after ... if!* one has been so lucky as to survive a shipwreck.

I am the topographical map of my environment ... a *slowly* changing map. What repeats, cuts. What is intense, cuts. Moreover, I carry the maps of the past into the present. In fact, I am not looking at maps of two dimensions, but a blending of many maps and many more dimensions than I can number: the five senses, the blood, the heart, the stomach ... to name a few. My "consciousness," therefore, is a fusion of past and present influences and impressions ... always a distortion of the current environment.

If I am ever to gain any sort of control over my own development, I must learn how to mold the topography on my own terms ... and the only way I can do this is to manipulate my surface world. This is no easy task, considering that I can never see this world perfectly.

Because my impressions are multi-layered and ever changing, my first step is to stabilize the surface world: eat well, reduce stimuli, simplify my environment, and get things to repeat to my advantage as much as possible. Ultimately, it is through *repetition* that I begin to finger the topography: altering the orbits of small and light objects one at a time. Gradually, the surface world and I shape each other.

I cannot bring "mind" or "positive thinking" into this. "Mind" is the backward thinking machine ... a jumbled memory. Mind, if reduced to anything at all, is merely that error-making organ, the brain. Put metaphysically, that is to say, as one error describing another, mind is the product of human vanity and fear. It *is* the ghost in the machine and as such, it does not exist.

It can be *believed*, however ... in the same sense that the audience believes in a magician's gimmick. One such useful trick is no longer to posit "mind" as in control ... but to see "mind" as inert clay, spinning on a wheel ... to see the surface world, that immediate, amoral, material world *as mind* ... the future mind ... outside. Thus, mind, to repeat, is not "inner," not "thought," and certainly *not* in direct control. If one has any control at all, it lies in mastering reverberations ... but then one does not need "mind" for that! *Hands* are more to the point ... those beautiful instruments which alone can shape the clay. Here, for once, real progress! ... and so easy, soft ... life had never been so workable! But to command the clay to shape itself! To "think" oneself out of misery ... to discuss ... when a simple ingredient added or removed would be *infinitely* more beneficial! As infinite as the distance between something and nothing is infinite! A glass of water, for example.

Preferring Stimuli

363

How I let go: I pick up something else ... or even better, I have something thrown to me at a key point of the day.

364

He points the prow toward the shore because he likes to feel the wind on his face. Never mind that as the wind blows his world grows smaller by the hour. Never mind that he will never set foot on solid ground. Never mind that he renounces a greater joy simply because he will not tack against a lesser one.

365

With the majority of topics it is a compliment to have one's ignorance exposed.

366

Everywhere, the stimulus presents itself to the human subject as something substantial, something solid.

367

I am both bell and dog, but never Pavlov.

368

The aim is control, and to be in control, I must control the frequency of contact with key stimuli.

369

The morning works for those who become someone in their sleep. The evening rebuilds and settles them into usable layers. Others need the morning for this rebuilding and settling ... need the hundred or so public stimuli before anything can happen at all.

370

I can *march* or I can *dance*. It all depends on whether I *decrease* or *increase* with a stimulus.

371

The louder the criticism the more I want to know of it? As if the best place to hear cannon fire were directly in front of it?

372

How can I feel myself threatened again with a choice I have *already* made? In reality, I have not chosen until I carry along something new or leave behind something old *for a sufficient length of time* ... and this *something* is not one half of the "choice," but the physical object that stimulates this new, competing desire.

373

Once things begin to redeem themselves I have to be careful of that which I make contact. Euphoria refuses to distinguish between the grand and the mediocre.

374

If I have not removed myself from the stimulus in question, I am opposed or compliant. Either way I am beyond help. My proposed destination is point *A*, but the immediate stimulus only provides the choice between destinations *B* and *C*. Every morning I grit my teeth and pull down my brow before the problem and every day my jaw falls as I watch myself pass, helplessly, by my higher destination ... *and all because I still respect the primacy of thought.*

375

We declare war by our response to the most recent stimuli, recruited *for* or *against*, but surrender to our oldest habits.

376

I live by many lights of many different colors, and my world reveals itself accordingly. However, by extinguishing a few of the colors now and then, I can see more of my world. For example, red cannot be seen but through the sufficient abatement of red light. And in just this way, a deep love can be obscured with prurience. This love cannot even be seen under a too bright and constant *pure* love, but must suffer an abatement now and then ... as a pulsating star thus reveals itself and becomes the wonder of the entire galaxy.

377

Managing life by way of stimulus and response can look so much like superstition as to confuse even the manager — if, for example, he sees only a limited portion of the vast number of influences or if he confuses a minor influence with a major. He has to remind himself constantly of the legitimacy of the effort ... but in doing this he looks something like the man who walks through a graveyard under a full moon, alone and repeating to himself, "I don't believe in ghosts. I don't believe in ghosts."

Becoming

378

An Attempt: To strike this vague, blunt end such that I force my point forward and part the two sides of error, the two extremes of the matter, to send them flying off beyond my periphery and out of view ... proud in what remains: the sharp, and recently burnished, point.

379

Those who hold the highest value shape themselves over time. They are blacksmiths of the body, not thinkers.

380

I cannot both agree to change and to remain myself. One of us must die.

381

Every valuable act is a fight away from the influence of immediate and bright stimuli and toward distant and self-redeeming repetitions.

382

We are built with the countless atoms of our petty moments.

Often a great act is not as great as it is the confusion of our times that is great. We seem to require ... even crave the confusion, have a vested interest in gripping and holding back the ever flowing tendencies of nature with monstrous demands: "Nature must be that. I command it not to be this."

We all have our doubts and fears and want a certainty secured, fixed in time and space, something to cling to so as not to be swept away into the uncertain. And so in great or small acts we grip and hold back what would otherwise flow on nobly according to its own law of becoming.

This "certainty" stands as a giant monolith in the great river of time, not stopping so much as flooding and stripping away the surrounding soil, striking out into jagged forks what had until then been coming together ... what would have remained tributaries toward a simpler, grander force are now trickling streams and stagnant puddles.

What is it that we "believe"? That repetition is boredom ... that we must and can *escape* the natural tendency to finish where we begin.

This escape ... this false "certainty" *is* the confusion on whose behalf we cling to immovable measures which fix that very confusion into place ... and for which ... in such a panic, we cling to our monolith all the more fervently, that being the "great" and "immovable" Savior.

By ruler and pen, we etch out our goals in straight lines, from point *A* to point *B*, today and tomorrow and thereafter ... never seeing that this *today* and *tomorrow* is, in the greater view of things, part of a greater circle, whose points *A* and *B*, this straight line, are but a single small point along infinite points of a great cycle, spiraling up toward an unintended and unseen point *C*. Thus, when I walk from point *A* to point *B*, two journeys take place: one of space and one of evolution — the linear journey completed in its thousand steps *horizontally* included a *vertical* step — a higher destination.

It is the truly great act in life to simplify one's own circumstance: with one command, to let go of this fixed monolith to chaos, have this letting go settle one's existence into comprehensible layers ... to resist all that would stop and have sensory objects fixed in place. In this, we seem contrary to nature, even while in our most natural state, for we resist those leaden desires which all others believe imperative and certain. We grip the only valuable reality, the ultimate truth, the light of all things: *repetition*, also known by the name of its consequence, *becoming*. But to place this one jewel firmly within our grip, we must empty our hand of all else.

Our "stopping place" is with the *flow* of the river, as a bark which floats downriver is fixed to the flow, and for this we cut loose every certainty and desire which would moor us to our own times.

384

A valuable book may be torn to pieces without diminishing the human spirit, just so long as the words have already been read and understood. To feel the loss of the book — at its material destruction, even though one had already digested its contents fully and had aligned oneself toward its overall direction — is evidence that one values the *non-human being* over *human becoming*, the static *thing* over the dynamic *process*. In response to the fear of our unknowable future we would rather freeze ourselves into a single stage of growth at the expense of the entire metamorphosis.

An eye for the *spirit of human becoming*, however, would find innumerable subtle devices, which would appear static, but which over time would prove their great worth to the process of the human spirit. For example, the chair does more than the desk; food, more than the plate it is served upon; a physical affection returns more than an *ideal* love which *pours itself through a sieve*, believing itself exempt from the need for physical touch, and so becoming unknowingly duplicitous. Nonetheless, let me qualify the previous observation. A true love desires the return of physical touch, that *return* being of more value than any single instance of touch, and yet, in itself impossible without each and every touch.

The human spirit is this pleasure in the accumulation, the *return* of delighting in the exhibition of one's strength and beauty, distinguished from vice, which merely *wants* to return, but cannot, whose entire "process" is one of stops and beginnings ... each stop a collapse from exhaustion ... each beginning requiring more than the available strength and health.

Of human spirit nothing is known of beginnings and endings, but all things necessary to the process are completed. As the rolling wheel, each point, though seen and proven to stop and touch at a particular point on the ground, does not by that very observation stop the wheel.

385

The velleity, *the Independent Repetition*, must be invited into the foreground. It comes when permitted but will not be manipulated. All that is required is the elimination of every extremity. To desire any single thing more than the ascending repetition is to stop that repetition and fly apart into chaos. We may appear very much like the old ascetic, yet the art of repetition is not an act of self-infliction or atonement: to delight in every good thing ... to find it distilled and bottled into a quintessence is our goal, and for this we must crave above all other things the *exalting repetition*. Our "conscious control" over nature is only our avoiding the unnatural and permitting *repetition* to organize our world on its own.

Art and Beauty

386

If one asked the man on the street — "What is genius?" or, "Who do you consider *a genius?*" —one would soon find that all of their answers have one common trait: a worshipping of *specialization* ... which is everything *but* genius. Now, I do not wish to be one of those cowards who reveal all that *"is not"* without venturing into the more precarious exploration of revealing what *"is."* So, what then is *Genius?*

Genius is the effort against one's natural inclination to specialize and against the cheap gratification of easy and quick demonstrations of potential. Perhaps I am a coward after all, for my definition ... my process is no different from the coward's smug assertions. Well then, genius is *that* case where one man's courage is another's cowardice: after eliminating what genius is not I am left, by default, with a vague description of what *genius* is: a perfect sphere ... a totality. Genius is the result of the daily *refusal to specialize* ... *the refusal* to sacrifice oneself as a public spectacle ... and yet even the refusal to isolate oneself from *all* intrusions and accidents.

This *isolation,* the desire to protect one's creation, seems to be an absolute necessity for the modern artist, often confused with true genius. *Isolation* increases sensitivity. Sensitivity is the heart and soul of an artist. The artist, like any other human, craves of course what it lacks: happy accidents, other people, family. However, the object of this hunger is never set upon the table, but a substitute — a more refined dish — is prepared: the *work of art* ... the substitute ... which in turn requires further isolation, for the digestion of this "dish" is not easy. The artist then feeds upon himself, one of his own organs serving as parasite to all of the others. His totality ... *his* health sacrificed for the hypertrophy of one single, grand talent. The modern artist ... what has been regarded thus far as the artist is a monster.

Something here ought to be said of the artist's patrons ... the modern consumers. What do they want? Nothing less than the spectacle of the artist's complete self-sacrifice in the arena. Any gladiator who would merit a "thumbs up" upon defeat *and who would accept the reprieve,* to them, is no artist. No, the consumer's hunger must be gratified, and yet his conscience must remain clean. He must grant the reprieve and then leave it up to the would-be artist to decide whether or not to merit the title. The artist, it follows, must be defeated and then must refuse all options that do not result in his immediate and complete destruction, the "thumbs up" opening the way to the last and "ultimate sacrifice" of the artist. That which marks the completion of the work then has nothing to do with the work itself and everything to do with the circumstance of the artist: a "refusal" whose *direct* consequence is self-destruction, thereby "proving" the power of an ultimate and *free* choice.

387

Are the children pretending to be cormorants more beautiful than the birds themselves?

388

It does not matter how well we hammer our gold into dishes. The fruit still rots. Better to eat the peach now and to hammer our gold into something hard enough for time. Quick and enduring pleasures ... for there are none in between.

389

So much accident and innocence need to collide together to form a single, rare beauty that one always ruins the process when one knows what to do ... yet it is this knowing that we crave.

390

The end of Art is Beauty: to rearrange the world so that it becomes seductive again ... as a surface. For Beauty *is* only skin deep. It is my breast that acquires depth.

391

Beauty was at first anthropomorphic. And then after we built a second step for our art, pulled it further away from the human, it was not un-anthropomorphic ... or *objective* ... it was just less beautiful.

392

A forgotten truth, three flowers, each of a different color and fragrance ... the sight and scent, where even the silence contributes and I need not touch to feel the pleasure. For only where the senses blend and let be, where I refuse to separate, can there be joy.

393

We take art to be something alien to our nature, something *above* science, something that resists the laws of mechanics or is at least destroyed by them. We think that there is a fundamental difference between the art and the artificial. But there was an age that thought differently. There was a time when the word, "art," was a blood relative to the word "artificial." The confusion began when we stopped *making* art. Now, our modern artists, make ideas. The work of art, they would have us believe, is incidental to the philosophy.

394

Genius begins with the discovery that there is always an art to the magician's trick and never a magic to the art.

395

We must appropriate and never borrow. We predatory creatures do not have enough stomachs to be scholars. We have been perfectly adapted to digest our experiences with the first pass. Who among us would be so indecent as to bring up the idea in its original form? Who cares for "original" ideas at all? Only *the experience* of the idea can sustain us ... and that has more to do with *us* than an "originator."

When I look at my leg, I do not see a carrot. Before I leap, I do not first give credit to a potato. The muscle is mine. The energy is mine. The movement is mine. I am the sum total of all my experiences, and with the absorption of each new "idea," this dance also becomes *mine*.

The confusion arrives when we imagine ourselves as the cows of scholarship, our task being to ruminate old ideas into news ones ... to focus upon and extend the digestion process for as long as possible ... and then, when finished, to find the *potential* of the animal irrelevant.

396

On the indecent honesty: We all use the same naked truths, but very few clothe and groom them well enough for their courtship with eternity.

397

Let us leave alone that modern, false logic: reality is sometimes disgusting; therefore when I show the disgusting, I show reality.

398

It is a blunder to construct a clever metaphor first and then to look for something to do with it. The art is to look for power in the human universe and then have *it* find something to represent itself.

That which makes the metaphor is the same which makes the avalanche, *accumulated force.* There is a point in the creation of a metaphor where there is nothing more I can do; it *will* fall! ... but how far back is that point? And how do I *make* it fall?

But to contradict myself ... and perhaps not to contradict myself ... the *avalanche* metaphor was not my initial choice. The first image to float to the surface was ... a beach ball ... imagine *that* next to "force." So I sat and flipped through three other images, each representing the law of force: a lever, a pulley, an avalanche. I chose *"avalanche"* because of its accidental nature, which, in today's technological world, is slowly falling under our *control.* The reader could argue successfully that *"avalanche"* was not very spontaneous and that it contradicts the fundamental effort of this passage, but I could also counter that the avalanche was just a few images back ... that when I grabbed hold of the first image I *precipitated* several others.

This represents my entire effort in writing: not nature so much as *force in nature* ... not merely to calculate, *but to precipitate* ... to line up the undulations of tendency such that they overlap and threaten the very coast of presumption. We are enemies, my sea against this coast ... desires crashing against seemingly inexorable Facts and Laws. I do not wish to stand firmly upon my "certainties" ... but to *foretell* and *precipitate* that rare moment when time will pull down the rugged certainty from under me and lay it gently into the sea.

Toward Victory

399

The promise of victory pleases us ... as much, if not more than the victory itself.

400

If I have not made an advance in a long time, in spite of a great effort, I conclude that I have *never* made an advance. A single victory and I am settled again, relaxing beside my trophy laden fireplace.

401

A strategy without adequate resources has little chance for victory, but that says little of the strategy itself. Many who have failed have had their plans buried with them, only to have the lesser plan of a lesser architect adopted — and all because fate was a poor instructor, because of the human tendency to magnify chance points of victory or failure such that they dwarf the greatness ... the *eventual* victory of a superior plan, however weak its resources at the moment.

402

One does not chop around the entire circumference of the tree; one chips away at one place.

403

The question is not whether or not I am capable. Very few people are incapable. The question is whether or not I return to my coign of vantage after each exploit.

The Human Spirit

404

The anatomy of the Human Spirit:

The inner man takes a step back away from things ... and attempts to visualize *relationships,* between himself and things, himself and others, but chiefly, between his "inner" and his "outer" self.

The outer man is concerned with *things* and people only, which he does not see as *thing desired* ... *thing* and *desire* are inseparable from *him*. His movement depends upon his taking each step for granted. He would never ask himself, "Why do I desire this?"

The inner man is the thwarted man. He questions his desire for what he cannot have ... so as to eliminate the desired object from his equation of himself ... or at least to "go around" his "miscalculations" of low self-esteem.

The outer man is the potentate. His path *is* clear. Why place the obstacle of a question in his own way? Why stop for an equation? Questions and equations are for going around obstacles, but if there are no obstacles? Would not the question and the equation, as longer routes, *become* obstacles?

The Inner man is the perfect servant. He has no direct path to his own object. He has no Will of his own, and of the Will that is *granted* to him, he must first justify and explain before he can act — or receive yet another confirmation from an even *higher* authority. He must conciliate *and* compromise ... or find new and higher rules. Consequently, every simple task or aspect grows ... every solution complicates ... yet serves as gauge to *his* own spirituality, as proof that he has grown more intricate, delicate. He himself becomes an invaluable instrument of precision for measuring the universe.

The outer man cannot see these "frills" and "extra baggage" of the inner man without rolling on the ground with laughter. He has

129

one Will only ... for he does not see his contradictions while passing from one moment to the next. Consequently, he is no hypocrite. He is the supreme ruler, the conquistador. His tendency is toward oversimplification — his anatomy for example: his hand and brain are of one single organ.

405

To grow intellectually is to contract and expand, to create and destroy. This ecstasy and suffering ... this conception and labor give birth to another joy, what we call "spirituality."

Conscience and Decision

406

The object of every new experience: To make it worthy of the memory.

407

The thrill is in the hunt not the kill ... but there is no hunt without the kill.

408

I gain always at the expense of innocence, and I feel the loss as I feel all losses ... with regret and resentment. But let me learn how to be ashamed of this innocence and not its loss ... as the boy learns after his first hunt, that the kill raises the hair on his nape, that there is exhilaration behind the guilt ... and that this exhilaration is older and stronger.

I have inherited all of my presumptions from my culture, so if I find that I have erred, how can I blame myself? On the contrary, I ought to celebrate the removal of the error *and* feel relieved that I lack all accountability.

Where does that leave me? Two steps ahead ... I have dropped an error and no longer go back for it.

410

"If I only knew then what I know now." But regret is also proof that one has evolved ... that one looks down, not upon oneself, but upon one's former self, as if at a lower species.

411

I have created for myself imaginary peers. Every act is brought before their judgment. It is an involuntary, perhaps vain, daydream ... but it is *functional*. I have control over the choice of these imaginary peers ... and their banishment.

This may sound childish — it certainly *appears* childish — but I surround myself with the pictures of new peers and read only the works of these new peers. To banish, I only need tear down a picture and avoid all contact with any hint of their existence. The process is slow and more easily reversed than advanced, but it works.

In the twentieth century, do we still have to say it? Conscience is plastic.

412

My categorical imperative: If my next act were to become a habit for life, would it make me stronger or weaker?

Truth is a hammer, and society has secured the crown jewels in a glass case. What should I do? What should I do? ...

Magic and Sensation

"I have dark areas? But how else can I have depth? How else can I *avoid* this one blinding truth: that every depth illuminated becomes surface again."

We wanted the *real* truth and when we had finally found it, we realized that we had also become mad in the process ... that it was precisely this madness that we had been seeking all along. Now, in our too bright, shadowless world, our metaphysical aspiration toward a higher honesty has revealed itself at last in substance and form *as a disease of the nervous system*. We search for one last shadow in order to shut our eyes again, to sleep for a spell. We awake into a new world striped with darkness ... in joy find that we have again risen above the surface of things.

To *"think"* one's way out of a miserable situation is to leap into a vacuum for lack of oxygen. We all think too much, all in our "mental" miseries, squirming in place, when we could move a few simple objects, change a single habit, *walk five paces* into an entirely new world. With a flick of the wrist, we could use the error-making organ to our advantage ... redeem our everyday world into a paradise ... render all our past sufferings indispensable to current joys.

Looking down on a valley from a restful state, one that required no sacrifices, is not the same as looking down on that same valley from a height acquired through sacrifice ... from a distance of exhilaration. One viewer never fully understands the other, yet each presumes that they each share the same wonder or boredom.

Along these same lines, within a single human, the error-making organ is incapable of leaning on its next state ... does not even believe in its existence. From one moment to the next, one can pass through tremendous leaps of the "spirit" ... a single letter in the mail, for example, can send one floating toward bliss or sinking into despair. This current frame of reference, filled or emptied of the stuff of life, is both the beginning and the end. That we are in a *new* room is certain, but we fail to find a door.

There must have been times when a human has, out of despair, decided to end life by leaping from a tall building. By the time he reached the uppermost floor, however, his physical exhilaration had risen to such a degree, his reasoning powers had been operating at such a higher level that he had in fact become a different species ... for whom the original problem was no longer relevant. Presently, he is happy and *secure* ... since in this room too he finds no doors.

417

The object is to get the illusion to hover as closely to the surface as possible, since that is where the energy is. To put it another way, *only the surface can increase the value of the illusion.*

418

The temptation: I cannot reach beyond the length of my arm, but it is flattering, and even useful, to have others believe that I can.

419

I am long past trying to see *behind* the fact or wanting the idea to separate from and levitate *above* the fact. The sentence is not the magic, but the lovely assistant. She knows and sees the sleight of

133

hand ... *stands beside* the fact and helps the illusion succeed. At best, magic is a trick and only as such does it convince.

420

There is no soul, and yet we have our words. There is no magic, and yet we have become magicians. Perhaps it is the thrill of deception, of taking in, not only the audience, but *ourselves as well*. We lift our brows before the sleight of our own hands ... forget our own mirrors, lighting and shadows ... and then one day, we look the girl in the face and hesitate, the saw in our hands, and she, doing her best to mask a fear.

421

After seeing the magician's mirror for the first time, one is *not* necessarily disappointed. On the contrary, one can be fascinated with the deception ... take delight *in the hunt* for these mirrors and trap doors. One even frequents these popular shows, not for the entertainment of the act, but for the entertainment of *exposing* the act ... but by this time one is no longer granted admission.

422

One has to know *instinctively*, and not *consciously*, of the sleight of hand necessary for magic. This may help to explain why the honest man is so clumsy when he tries *his* magic: he has not the instinct, and feels he has to roll up his sleeves and *expose* all of the secrets. He feels a certain pride in this exposure ... and with good reason, for how *cleverly* he disappoints his audience! However, as in most of life's affairs, one will always go farther if one studies the magician *for the magic* ... for sleight of hand. *What the other does not see makes the magic.* A little diversion goes a long way here ...

In a world where I permit no magic, all becomes a gimmick. The fall from the magical to the mechanical is great ... but the audience will wait for that fall. This is the lure of magic: it walks that tightrope between the impossible and the possible. If it does not fall, we wonder. If it falls, we may even watch with more intensity for the next theatrical disaster; it entertains us.

The magician can repeat his magic for as long as he wishes and entertain us, but the moment he intentionally reveals the mechanical nature of the performance ... the moment the elastic reach for the impossible snaps back into the possible, he has performed this piece of magic for the last time. Now imagine a performer who showed only the mechanical! Even the *comedy* of the performance would wear on us. How could we bear to await the end? So, a good magician never shows the mechanical. If we happen to see through the magic, well, he always has another trick up his sleeve. This will keep even the most astute observer on the edge of his seat. Fortunately, in this regard, nature has been the greatest of all magicians.

Prophecy

It could be argued that we do not really have a concept of the future; we simply learn the repetition of past events. We translate *what was* into *that which will come around again*. What we call our future is nothing other than the sum total of our past. We fit into this repetition just as a needle of a phonograph fits into the groove of a record. In time we gain an extraordinary and blind confidence in the repetition of events. When this blindness is comfortable and convenient, we call it *Free Will*.

Of course, it follows then that if a man has not seen the repetition in his life, he must necessarily deny what has just been said here and with proof, for it is only obvious to him that he does in fact have *Free Will*. Everything he wishes to happen, happens!

It is not however obvious to me at all. My *Free Will* is only the acknowledgment of but one more cog in the machine: How did I wish precisely this? ... and most importantly, can I manipulate my repetitions in such a way that I elevate my wishes?

425

A thought can race on ahead of the act, but it can do nothing in that future. As we all know, action lies only in the here and now, and it is near that fixed point, where thought is needed the most, and where it has too little influence.   Thought, to be truly effective, must serve as trainer, must drill, if it is to have the totality of the man react at the opportune moment toward a desired effect.   And here, in knowing what to do, one can argue that it is not a *leaping ahead*, but a *looking back* on past experience, recognizing that an experience will repeat in a similar way, and that the task is to manipulate some key element in that repetition. Our thoughts of the future, of prophecy, are divined from the entrails of our past repetitions.

Spontaneity

426

Note the difference between the spontaneity of the popular "transcendentalist" and that of the behaviorist. The one stands "impromptu," *pushing* the issue with the best of intentions, but who, like the hand in the clear pond, upsets the sediment and can no longer see into the depths of the matter ... or he makes an attempt at "pure thought" which disdains all "gimmicks" and so waits and waits, cursing the long intervals between revelations. The other avails himself of every sort of preparation — no matter how petty or ridiculous — and is *pulled* toward the object. [*]

[*] "But this is not spontaneity!"

... "Well then, nature is the more accomplished liar."

"So you then admit to your dishonesty?"

... "But sir, it was not we who began with the attempt to get beyond nature. We see spontaneity as the exploit of nature and not its escape, but if you insist, we will yield to your accusation — without compunction — for we enjoy this apple all the more for having "stolen" it."

427

Does One Proceed "Spontaneously" or Circumspectly? I side with circumspection, which takes into account the development of the human and his ability to succeed in future, unknown exploits. An untrained impulse takes into account only the exploit ... at the expense of all required to hone necessary skills.

Spontaneity requires too much luck and throws away much wisdom that could be learned if one would just pause and calculate a little. Thus, in an impulsive act, which is successful, a man may seize the prize, but at the expense of increased strength and wisdom ... and he is less likely to succeed in future endeavors. Not having taken into account the role of habits, he always seems to be carried away and fighting against the current. Eventually his arms tire, and he yields to the turbulence.

The circumspect man marches side by side with his accumulating exploits ... and he marches toward a *calculated* spontaneity ... one which grows more and more frequent ... both the human and the exploit adding to each other's luster and strength.

The Spirituality of Repetition

428

God is that single tendency worthy of all my life's effort.

429

Only the great invisible God, the God which has no other gods before it — repetition — can save. As far as I can see from here, it is the only reality capable of worship. It is the only reality which reconciles "mind" and "the immediate surface." It is not a third reality next to the immediate and the illusory, but is the bridge across the two. It is where and how they overlap. It makes "mind" necessary to the reality. All other perspectives fail. The "mind" alone is quixotic. The "immediate" is incomprehensible and leaves one desperate and humiliated. Repetition has the simplicity and strength to recline in beauty but which nonetheless remains incorruptible.

430

When we reach the state where all adjustments are petty, where we no longer seem to be building, but merely picking up after ourselves, *yet find ourselves ascending,* then we have *faith.* We are close. Formerly, we had no energy for reality, yet fancied we could move mountains.

Compensation

431

While it is true that good luck intoxicates: One thinks backwards ... always vainly, as in *I did this,* or *I was like this and therefore I was rewarded.* It is also true however that misfortune sobers. Disaster crushes all scaffolding to the ground. One stands again upon the unyielding surface world and no longer builds oneself upon promises or fortune. One has at last found something solid to stand on ... is perhaps even grateful.

432

Disappointment, one absolutely must pass through the eye of this needle if one is to live within the walls of a harder reality.

433

Disappointment is proportionate to desire and hope. It has nothing to do with the actual scope of the enterprise. A man can suffer greatly over a rotten garden tomato.

434

Only "mind" perceives a whole and that "mind" is an error. When it ceases to err, when this hollow vase shatters against an unyielding reality, the heavens themselves seem to fly apart and our sky is littered with shards. But soon we make our universe whole again ... rise above our own species and secure the perfect movements of our stars. That is to say, of the two, we lean toward the more beautiful madness.

435

I may very well have no new, bright and shining hopes but will keep these few old and unburnished certainties.

436

The Public Truth: In victory, we accept the bestowal of meaning and elevated purpose.

The Private Truth: In defeat, we console ourselves that loss is ultimately meaningless and impermanent.

Public: What is added unto me, makes me richer.

Private: What is taken away, deepens me.

438

Everyone perhaps has the same degree of difficulty: if it is not an outright opposition, well then it is our own complacency.

439

One cannot be a hero in one arena without being thought a coward in many others.

440

My discontent with myself? And he wants to remove it from me? What, after I finally have hook and barb to catch new ideas?

441

Dignity only shows its face to *loss.* A man in victory is not all that different from a buffoon.

442

Compensation by perspective: There is no mercy in nature, but then only the ignorant think of nature as "cruel."

443

The drive to *excellence* is an overcompensation for an unfathomable deficit — just as could be the *meanness* in us. We hold out before us a counterweight, some sort of ballast, without which we would fall over. It matters little which of the two we hold out: great or mean, we balance just the same. Yet because it matters little, and because we must hold *something*, why hold to meanness?

Providence

444

I have pursued the shell of existence ... and it is not despair. Those who have found only despair here are those who embraced the shell *in order to preserve the vacuum*. Let it fill ... let it fill ... it takes no effort to let it fill.

445

What never ceases to amaze me: how most people are not concerned in the least with an aim in life and yet seem content.

446

There are not so many choices as we would suppose, and we profane those few which remain. We believe that *pushing* an issue to its conclusion is a choice, wherein *allowing* the issue to develop on its own, favorably, is the least tenable but most substantial "choice." We "intend" an outcome to an event — like nymphs who stop up their ears so as to take sole credit for the dance, but who thereby are no longer *dancing*.

Unstopping the ears and waiting for the music are the more substantial choices. We dance by our *not* "willing" too much. *This* choosing ... this getting out of one's own way must require more discipline and preparation than one can endure, for why else would we have so few dancers?

447

I am paddling up the river, the debris rushing past me so strongly and swiftly that I believe I move *up* the river ... whereas I am

141

merely *struggling forwards* but *driven backwards by the strong current.* To turn my boat around would be the more enlightened approach. I would drift at the same speed as the debris under the new illusion that I am not moving at all.

I have an aggression that has finally learned to yield so that it may gain. It therefore *appears* passive.

From the Diary of the Megalomaniac

448

Where clarity does not accompany, pride will always exist as both solution and problem. Pride is like a pistol; it can arm police and criminal alike.

449

To favor pride at the expense of clarity, or even clarity at the expense of pride is to favor one leg, to limp.

450

Ninety-nine percent of the effort toward *life* is to permit a single ambitious thought.

451

Ambition can fill any moral vacuum ... and for a happy few, it can even burst it. No small wonder, since it was the public morality which had ripped our ambitions out of our breasts.

452

A formula for existence: A *Me*-science wired to a *We*-science and strapped to Energy, which *increases* with natural repetitions. Then upon this crudely jointed frame stitch on a skin of vanity ...

and through the ear implant raw ambition deep into the brain —
and then I have it, the creation of a life. Monstrous? Yes ... but
life nonetheless.

453

If reason truly governed humanity then we would clasp our hands
together and alternately bewail and respect the fact of our
existence. As it is we are a clamoring marketplace of self-interest,
and here, at least, a little happiness seems possible.

454

The only way to be rich and not be envied is to be poorer still than
everyone I know.

455

A dilemma would arise if the modern artist had to choose between
fame and wealth. If he were *certain* either of complete obscurity
or poverty, he would probably not continue. Of course, there is no
such dilemma, for he has too much respect for the mechanical
force of either to believe that such an exclusive choice would ever
be forced upon him.

456

Why fear ridicule? If my life's task proves to be unworthy, why
then, like most everything else in this world, the ridicule will pass
away.

If it proves to be worthy, why then ...

457

Only *fighting for gain* and *fighting against loss* have meaning.
But excuse my archaic use of the language here. In a much older
era, before we desired the *meaning of the thing* more than the

thing itself, we understood one another better and had no need to define the meaning of *"meaning."* Ambition.

458

We would march toward purity of heart but that we are always sliding toward our ambitions. To have both authenticity *and* joy, we conclude, we must first reclaim our ambitions with a proud heart.

459

Ambition is our love for *this* reality.

460

It is not *ambition* that ruins us, but the *smallness* of our ambition.

461

Those who speak against ambition do so by speaking down or up. Those who have it, speak down, for they want no competitors, and those who do not have it, speak up, for they want no one to remain above them.

There is a third species who do not denounce ambition, but remain silent, knowing that the word "ambition" could not uphold the very personal, and therefore *exalted*, expectation.

462

I can not see anything greater than this ... no higher ambition possible: to resist all that promises me more than my condition and to resist all that would have me settle for less. I stand up and shed no more tears, for between these two stone walls, at last, *I see my gate.*

463

Those two which survive the contradiction — repetition and surface reality — are the only remaining universals. In times past we stood securely, somewhere between the two ends of this spectrum, but all too many times since, we found ourselves suddenly upon a single, very fine point ... too small even to include us. This is the universal death of the honest mind and the birth of an existence — not that despite all our reasoning against ourselves we cannot deny our identities, but that this undeniable identity nonetheless constitutes our final blunder. This is a gloom that only a worldly ambition can brighten: whenever I think of the absolute futility of my life I instantly reconcile myself to my condition by plotting to conquer *my* world. Why not? Perhaps the world could even unite by making a new religion of its own conquest.

464

One who is so overcome with an exalted stimulus that one will endure all suffering on its behalf will become strong and holy. One who goes so far as to risk all — loss of reputation not the least and death not the most — is hero, acclaimed and unacclaimed. The reward in life is in the sensation: if in nothing else, then in the sensation that one has somehow become, even if only in the imaginary approval of one's peers, sensational.

465

The ancients taught their children: *"Make your heart small."* This age teaches them: *"Be content with who you are."* From shrinking the heart, we have progressed to stunting its growth.

466

We are the last of the discontented ... and hold this to be our highest virtue ... a discontentment which one cultivates. That other thing, that whisper, "Accept yourself for who you are," what is that but the formaldehyde of the public clinic? ... where every germ has been sterilized ... even that germ of life, discontent, has been sponged away by the hairless hands of our public guardians.

467

Vanity is one of the germs of life, and as such, it is the future. It does not show me who I am, but inflates an image of myself and floats it away from me. I feel the loss and would take it back. I follow.

468

How does one go about convincing the vain of their vanity? And then, if successful, how does one convince these newly defeated and humbled creatures that they need this vanity after all ... only to a greater degree?

469

My humility: Finding the soft spot to pound hard.

470

The unfortunate: Those who are given enough room for comfort never question the mediocrity of their small kingdom.

471

To become so valuable that no one will ever want to lose any piece of me is, in the end, the highest redemption; in the beginning, an inexcusable offense.

472

Fame is not the object. It is not the refutation either.

This is my life. To provide even the weakest justification for my *own* existence is so deep of a *need* that I would hinder my very efforts *towards* life if I did not write, qualified or not, *for a reader.* And so I make my solemn oath here and now, if only within the sanctuary of my own vanity: *I will become my own monument.*

I hate this custom where one must prove one's humble origins or past failures before one can have a good conscience with an advance in the world. *Another sort of conscience* requires that one see everything in the past *as a privilege.*

I seek that state where everything I touch is already gold.

Having vanity without a mirror is much like those "great" thoughts which do not point toward real control.

The consequences of a spark can be great, but that does not therefore make the spark great. One must not only be flint and steel ... not even powder ... nor the explosion itself ... but also the restriction, the calibrated cylinder ... the shot ... most of all, *the aim.* And if one should miss, despite the utmost effort and care, it is still possible to be inconsequentially great, being adequately compensated by the sensation.

God would humble me, and so I must exalt myself.

Those who would have me "more positive" would have me proceed "without defeat." That is to say, when confronted with an opposition, a contradiction, I am to flee and count that distance from the struggle as "victory." I would rather stay and fight the good fight. Sometimes "I" win, sometimes this machine. But always with honor. Always holding my own. Always honest. Always finding *this* pride constructive.

"I am this and this and this too!" Deny this need to affirm oneself, deny that one makes oneself the priority over all other concerns and "this" extends itself into an infinitely complex equation. Yet there is some alleviation here, the process of expanding and contracting the equation leaves one with the feeling of "progress."

Imagine a human whose "stream of consciousness" thinks itself aware of its own reinforced drives ... imagine the human experience as a *river* with *pride*, which at every bend reproaches itself for obeying the law of gravity, reason being, that this simple law shows the river to be too simplistic, a mere reaction. This pride opposes every natural force ... ensconcing the river "safely" within dark and insidious complexities. Such a river turns inward and tunnels through the mountain, taking such inner pride in its complexity that "outer" ... real strength is riddled through and becomes so brittle it can no longer bear its own weight. The mountain collapses. No longer full and proud as mountain, but hollow and low as crater.

Imagine the same river, again with pride, but with such pride that it refuses to pamper itself with the luxury of fear ... not so simple as smug obedience, nor *merely* complex ... nonetheless taking pride in simplicity — *for the sake of life force.* I value the inexorability in the universe, for I take pride in the *mechanical* increase of my force *thereby.* Everywhere I see the forces of nature squandered and so divert and channel all lesser streams of tendency into one simplified effort ... swell high with pride because I have *contained* force. I delight too, in that moment of repair, when pride spills over.

Dignity and Nobility

481

Before, I swallowed the promise of dignity and kept it as a lump in my throat. Now, I bury my chin in my chest in order to speak with a lower voice. It is hardly a fair trade; my new friends do not compensate.

482

I am human and have all of the human reflexes. If a clown were to grow angry and strike me, I must defend myself and become the spectacle of the whole circus. The only solution, it seems, is to flee from this circus. I must have noble and dignified peers or I will remain small and petty. Dignity seeks dignity and will seek nothing else ... or it is nothing.

483

If I should suffer the worst of all possible consequences: There is something which alone belongs to me, and I am willing to consecrate it with the sacrifice of my very existence. This is the human paradox: one must be willing to sacrifice existence for the *value* of that existence, even though one will have no means with which to enjoy that value ... *but there is something in the struggle.* Let us call it dignity. I cannot attempt another definition. We set words to this *thing* to deepen it and our swarming definitions eat labyrinths out of our wooden breasts and we think we have something in exchange for this brittle existence. Then one day we are crushed to powder against our finality. But there is something in the struggle.

And what, then, is the worst of all possible consequences? No, it is not that sacrifice to futility, but that we are condemned to battle for this dignity against a host of clowns. Very well then, life *is* fair after all. The people will have their spectacle; I will have my dignity.

484

One could leave this land behind ... travel a great distance and *for years* in only the *hope* of finding someone noble enough to wage war upon. There is dignity in *this* patience: it struggles toward a greater dignity. Never mind that column of clowns marching after us. We will never stop, and so they will never catch us. This *is* how we defeat them.

485

Dignity, it seems, increases with every attempt to diminish it ... as when lightning ignites the forest, blackens the mountain, making it fertile.

486

Sometimes we find ourselves one step back for every step we take forward. Very well then, where we cannot advance, we can at least resist being sent backwards. And there is perhaps dignity in even an unsuccessful resistance ... enough to drive the "futility" out of our next step forward.

487

Just when our dignity comes under attack and we seem to have none to spare, we find and wear proudly that which the struggle throws upon us, as nothing wears dignity so well as composure in strife.

488

One can strive for greatness and fail ... and fail with probability. One can strive for a genuine dignity and succeed ... with certainty. And if we wed the two, what child is born? For his dignity forbids that he give up his highest ambition, and this ambition requires the dignified acceptance of his probable failure. So, how does the child of this union, this *genuine failure*, conduct himself? He is pricked with the failure of his ambition but makes his *querencia* on precisely this plot of ground. He refuses any justification other than that *he is here* ... that the earth under his feet is his to the end ... on the confidence that for as long as he holds onto dignity, the value, even of failure, increases.

489

What is nobility? One and foremost: health. Two: courage. Three: lucidity.

As for wealth, fame, and political power: That nobility can possess these badges does not preclude a fair number of bare chests. Yet nobility is still physical ... physiological ... a material possession ... but as a wedge is material. It *works upon* instead of being *worked by* the matter. It divides, yet cares not for the matter itself, nor for the categories it leaves behind. Here, in the noble, the "perfect angle" is that which provides the greatest mechanical leverage. Thus, it chooses the angle — always straight, direct, central. It only appears oblique because others have already split and fallen askew. *That which is split* remains complex and unmanageable ... but it matters little, for *that which splits* remains nobly simple ... remains our simple goal.

490

To be great without eminence — or even the prospect of posthumous eminence is the final temptation: can one live by the noble sensation alone?

Authenticity

If I am to see *beyond* anything, let it be an attempt to see beyond my own thoughts ... to make that educated guess at what is *not* beyond me — that is to say, to struggle with my reality and no longer flee from it.

How much of my condition I can grip depends first upon how much of the "beyond" I can bear to let go.

Without rest there is nothing genuine. All attempts to muster up that last drop of energy *get that drop* but leave the cup empty. Now, I only mimic the *pouring out* and begin to question the need for the cup.

Only overflowing proves genuine. I can train myself to fill and pour over. To remove myself from the metaphor and approach the clinical, let me say that energy and reflex are what we formerly called "the genuine." It is physiological, not ethical. I can train myself toward it: an intentional repetition toward the unintentional reflex ... a new "spontaneity" that is *not* more disappointing than the old "spontaneity" — since we now have a little more control over the process.

Acceptance lies in habituating to the unpleasant. To accept my unconditional death, for example, I only need to affirm my condition for a sufficient length of time. As with all things, the unpleasantness of disillusionment lessens with *repetition*. I then proceed to affirm my life ... to steer it from a stark authenticity to a cycle of increasing value.

"Virtue is its own reward," and by experience, one soon learns that virtue is never so restrictive but so expansive as to say, "Wherever there is a reward in which we are not duplicitous there is virtue."

The Struggle from Solitude

496

If everyone were found to walk exactly the same distance and to have exactly the same destination in life, then the manner of our travels would soon change. We would then compete with our *styles* of walking. To be human is to compare and contrast, always with the intent to outdo our neighbor ... and if we are able we will *continually change the object of the competition* in order to surpass each and every companion in each and every context ... for to be consistent with one single object in life would be to resign the majority of experiences to defeat.

However, if we could sum up all of our aims, observe how the several vectors of our several social contexts collide and resolve us into a single concluding aim ... a direction and force in life too far removed from the senses to be observed except as reconstructed on a chalkboard ... would not this give us the vision with which to adjust each and every vector in our day to a grand, triumphant aim? ... would it not redeem the petty losses of our petty contexts? But how do we keep this chalkboard in full view in each and every humiliating moment — in those contexts which are necessary, but beneath us — so that we do not veer off from our *grand* direction by reflexes which are all too natural to our species? For this chalkboard itself is dependent upon context: solitude.

What we formerly thought was a step toward solitude was really just a step *away* from weakness, which is to say that it was not really a step at all but a *turning around* so that we could take our first real step toward strength.

Now that we are in full stride again we are surprised with how many people accompany us. We look back and laugh at the number of people our former solitude required.

498

Out of Solitude: There was a time when I was drained of my life's blood by the leaches of pity and duty. Survival, it seemed to me, demanded that I refuse to wade through the swamp, but *pause* on the shore, standing with my arms folded and uttering refusal after refusal. It never occurred to me that I could walk *around* with a good conscience ... not to mention the pleasant company.

499

The goal is not independence or nonconformity, but to free oneself of error and then to march toward a high fate, deaf to the jeering or applauding crowds ... and enduring the silence.

500

A large part of our problem with friendship is our belief that we must keep our friends at any cost — and one such expense is the awareness that the "friendship" may not be genuine. This provokes two questions: *Can a relationship which stands between ourselves and our progress be genuine? What is it that we really want when we preserve a friendship which is not genuine?*

501

The solution to the human condition and to the problems of the world as a whole, lies not with the perfection of a logical equation or judicial system, but with cultivating and passing down tastes and habits. When culture is seen as a goal and not as an inheritance that we take for granted, then perhaps we can begin to march toward progress rather than continue to retreat from disaster generation after generation.

In the next great revolution, a new variation of our species will rip the pages from our law books and wave them before the world as the flags of blunder ... as the failures of our customs. This new species will, of course, be torn to pieces. Then a few others will see that laws do not matter much ... have never mattered much ... even as the evidence of blunder ... will see the lever jutting out of the darker half of the world, unmanned ... and forgetting the heap of books behind them, will grab hold and ...

The *Real* God

502

If there is a God, then there can only be one way to Him — and that does not *begin* with God, but with God's reality.

Mortality

503

The average life is a long, drawn out process punctuated with eternity.

504

There is no life after death and oddly enough that raises the value of life and deepens my sense for meaning.

505

I fear a sudden, "unfair" death, and yet this mortality also serves as a stimulus toward life ... a condition of an aggressive pursuit of more, much more life. I even become addicted to the pleasure of seeing things pass by ... like autumn ... or the face of a child ... or suffering. It is difficult for me to imagine a valuable life without death ... just as it must be difficult for those with "Immortal Souls" to do anything else but wait life out. To realize my spirituality, perhaps I even *need* to die.

506

Just as finishing his daily tasks helps him sleep at night, living well eases death.

507

Death is an indifferent neighbor, whose hedge creeps onto *my* property. *I* must trim it back at my own expense and effort ... and without complaint, for I must accept the encroachment of the hedge and forget this slight if I am to enjoy this neighborhood, this house, this life.

508

"There is *absolutely* nothing to fear since death is not a human experience," and so how do I account for my remaining fear? My fear, then, must be that which has been left out of the above logic. Fear must be a part of the human body, just as is a kidney or a finger. I can not reason away a kidney when it makes me suffer. I can however amputate it, just as I am sure that I could have some piece of my brain amputated so as to eliminate all fear. But what must *necessarily* be attached to that amputation? Would my courage be greater than that of the seafaring pig in the storm? How much more firmly do I stand through the opposition of gravity? How much the nobler am I with fears to oppose? How could such nobility be possible otherwise? I would even express gratitude for my death, but that it is also a point of honor never to yield an inch to an enemy ... and a dishonorable death is my enemy.

509

What is this talk of death? There are many willing to risk death for fame and glory, but few who can withstand, for five minutes, the ridicule of their peers ... yet only he who can withstand derision has a chance to master *life*. He who masters death masters death.

510

Let the bleary eyed stare at this corpse all night long. *I* would find my strings in the very darkness of the stage ... and, as my own puppet master, would have me *live*.

Eat, Drink, and Create ... and tomorrow we'll be the merrier! ... for what's to fear when we have no faculty for the experience of death. As far as *I* am concerned, *I* shall never pierce through the membrane of *this life. Nothingness* is only "thinkable." There are no riddles which are not also distractions. The art of life ... the art of creation! Evermore, the *act* of creation! Life is an orgy of experience. Let us so grace the world with our lives that we beg for nothing in return for our deaths.

512

Heaven is the next world in the sense of the next higher repetition of key circumstances. If we have learned to live *here*, then we will be more capable of living *there*. To confuse this worldly goal with an after-life is proof of one's reluctance to live *here*.

To translate my Christian metaphor: Heaven is the sudden ascension into and endurance of higher and higher contexts in this world. Hell is the ignorance of the process of God's creation (Nature) and the punishment is to slide backwards and downwards, every repetition a decrease in life force.

I could also use a Buddhist metaphor, but anyone who is already responsive to the original Buddha, Gautama, can already put the much later Buddhists' Transmigration into a *this-world* context and is in no need of further explanation — likewise, the self-behaviorist. Each context in *this life* is the new "other" world we seek.

513

My short-lived experiences with the "Eternal" ... the "universal": 1) the recognition of like-experiences, the confidence that we can reach a state, in this life, where our identity unifies with *past lives* — *not* "reincarnation," but more akin to finding *ourselves* accurately portrayed in Shakespearean drama; or 2) the creation of a work of art, the confidence that other future lives will also experience, independently, *our* highest states. I therefore "continue," in the sense that another, future self will have like-experiences, will look back and smile upon me, as though looking in the mirror.

Given such a choice, between a physiological immortality and the short-lived identification with a "timeless state," and despite every romantic attempt to embellish the latter, who would ... *could* really choose the ephemeral experience? We choose the ephemeral only because the loss of our identity seems unavoidable, because it is the only honest approach, but also because it consoles us in our highest state of awareness, namely, that our most valuable memories will be wasted. That others will also share this sense of genuine existence alleviates the suffering. A genuine relationship with reality, shared, is a slice of eternity, a flicker from my candle, from which others might ignite and carry our flame forward. Only in this sense can *I* continue ... and it is a difficult and painful redefinition of the word "I." It is also — and this carries us above mere "consolation" — a nobler use of the word "I" — for the flame requires the spark, our steeled *will* striking against real flint. In short, it requires a disciplined and valiant indifference to Fate.

514

That death does not add to nor subtract from the meaningfulness of our lives: I observe the world and find that what the average person considers *significant* is invariably a petty stimulus, a fear, a vanity, or inherited custom. A man speaks with great words, carefully delineating *what he lives by* ... then loses his job and suffers an emotional breakdown. Even the loss of electricity and water for one week would provoke an uproar among average "good citizens." Observe what happens to a man's value system were he suddenly deprived of his usual tobacco, beer, or coffee. There seems to be no limit to what we take for granted, because it is precisely *the limits* which we do indeed take for granted. One such limit is our inherited morality. I hear talk of the significance of a religion, but open my eyes and find the convenience of a ready-made morality, the security of a large group, and a shepherd. But the greatest misconception of significance lies with "immortality" — which is nothing but a fear disguised.

If we were immortal, would we not reach a state, even if eons from our present state, where we would conclude that all of the objects of our pursuits — our desires, revulsions, fears, indolences and resentments — proved meaningless? Would we then feel a need to be freed from the bonds of everlasting life? ... from an everlasting state of meaninglessness? ... from an infinite ennui? Not that the answer would then be to seek out our own deaths (Would not that be equally meaningless?), but to seek out a constructed course in life toward something "higher" — our lives becoming a *significance of* something higher — the marking of a trail which would seem to the younger, desire-bound immortals, as futile and a fate worse than death? ... not seeing that we too climb the steps of desire, that the lower desires are replaced by the higher ... and only from these higher levels can we see that the desires, revulsions, and resentments have been translated from *objects* into *processes* and *methods of self-transformation* ... that *these* desires are trustworthy and longer lasting. However, not seeing what we see, they conclude that we refuse *all* desire ... that because we do not respond in like manner to the same stimulus, we therefore deny ourselves *any* response. They believe that we deny ourselves a love for immortality, when in actuality we are only pursuing authentic lives and longer lasting joys ... finding immortality *irrelevant* to the acquisition of significance.

The removal of the desire for immortality constitutes *the* step higher. One step reached assumes that another must be left behind, and what is it really that we leave behind? An error ... the truth being that neither everlasting life *nor death* pertains to the essential problem of *this life*. Reality as we know it, with the single addition of immortality, would simply be a *re-interpretation* of the old problem, our insignificance rephrased: *"What is* significant *about this everlasting reality?"* Mere immortality, in the popular sense, would weigh upon our shoulders with an unendurable and everlasting ennui to such a degree that we would pray for the relief of mortality. Of course, we crave immortality — or rather, we *fear* mortality ... but my point is that this fear, this craving is irrelevant to our more valuable cravings and fears: that of significance and insignificance.

If, then, the *prospect* of everlasting life exalts *this mortal life* by existing as a rung on the ladder, and that we might climb all the higher only when we use and leave that rung behind, then nothing is left out and *immortality* finds its place within the human equation.

On the other hand, and I must admit it reluctantly, the end is perhaps *necessary*, but not to its own credit, and certainly not for anything which could come "after," but *necessary* as a point of reflection, as a positive stimulus toward *this life* ... just as the significance of a sentence requires a stop, which serves as a point of return — it limits and emphasizes all that has preceded. My whole life has both a beginning and a continuing, a tendency, but requires a stop ... a point from which I might propose a "forward" and a "backward," a point signifying a direction ... where another existence might begin. Without this stopping point, how could we signify a direction? How can a beginning, *point A,* manifest a direction without the existence of a *point B?* Indeed, from an even more important perspective, without the thousand thousand stopping places within my own brief life, what tendency of my own would be shown to my faculties of observation? What can be *my* significance *to myself* without my errors, without my stopping places?

In conclusion, a reference: Were Job to have been convinced that he had indeed been deprived of the assurance of Immortality, of an everlasting companionship with God ... he would surely, even at his lowest point, *have loved God* ...as he would have had none of that ingratitude which asks for more than this life, as he would thereby be loving *the gift of this life.* I find the depth of such an affirmation, which only *appears* as a renunciation, truly significant.

Who God is Not

515

Toward a healthier religion: The more authentic the stigmata of our saints, the more proof we have against them.

516

Hell is that place where I have to ask forgiveness in order to enter ... and then apologize for having to ask.

517

God is not the rip-cord I am to tape to my chest, nor is His religion a *story* of a parachute that will surely open when it is my turn to fall.

518

The dishonesty lies not so much in the belief of God as it does in the refusal to debate the right to the assertion.

519

Genuine Spirituality: Granted, there exist those rare individuals with genuine fear and trembling before the prospect of eternal consequences. But could we regard *fear and trembling* ... this *fleeing away* as a sincere attempt at the spiritual goal? The greater the coward the worthier the spirit?

Beyond the *horrors* of Christianity, could we not find at least a few attempts which are sincere and courageous? We protest, for we have seen sincere attempts to rise *higher*, beyond the drive to dominate other people ... beyond complacency, greed or fear. Does not this rare and nearly extinct species consistently *strive* for greater and greater *solitary* difficulties? "What could be more difficult than to *become* a sincere Christian?" becomes "What could be more difficult than the impossible?" They seek greater resistance to *prove* greater capability ... unto the point of finding the greatest resistance: "achieving the impossible." They want this *impossibility* even more than the eternal victory. They want superiority over themselves ... to become something higher ... *something fearless which will hold its ground against reality.*

This was the affirmative half of the seduction of Christianity ... *an attempt to draw on the Powers of Heaven.* The human species proved to be more insane than previously understood: it was the *impossibility* of Christ and Christianity that lured so many toward this abyss of futility. Those few it could not frighten, *it challenged.*

Now, if Christianity had been other than impossible ... if it had been downright easy ... if Christianity had been *the natural order of things,* it would have gone nowhere ... having nothing to resist, nothing to strive after, the goal requiring not a gripping of oneself but a *letting go,* the sincere would have become bored ... *with the reality.* "Then what do I wait for in this next life? ... yet more boredom?" They would *need* a danger to resist, would rather become the Antichrist itself than to succumb to this ennui. They would renounce ... *again!* ... *all reality* just so as to strive after *yet another impossibility with which to prove that they are still fearless.*

520

Every honest approach to God must start with *who God cannot possibly be.* What one ends up with is not the God of an institution, nor that of another world, nor that which fits easily into the word, "God." Looser fitting clothing are required: "The sum of the life experience." Or, "What in life is worth living." "The exclusively human perspective in a demonstrably *non-*human universe." Somewhere in the overlap of these truths there is "God."

God is bold, not weak. God does not cower before bold and honest questioning. God does not vanish with disbelief or antagonism. God does not garner in brow-beaten slaves. God's chosen are not the lowly, not the meek, not the sick. God is the noble in us ... the resistance and not the compliance. God is this Human Spirit ... that within us which stands up what would otherwise fall down. So let us never again prostrate ourselves before an institution ... a book ... a history ... another human. Let us be great ourselves ... for the real God shall only be seen by the godly ... in a glass ... and face to face.

The Name of God

522

God, truly understood, would "set one free" ... even of "God."

523

In this chapter, I indulge in the "divine word set."

This shift is mostly one of word choice, with only a slight change in direction. My goal is still to affirm *this* reality ... to affirm *my* reality. My hope is that this section will be passed over by those who are seeking "other worlds" and that only those interested in an authentic orientation toward existence will have made it thus far. I expect this section to be rejected by atheists and believers alike. In short, anyone who prefers "reaction" to "clarity" — anyone who still believes in the magic of words — can and will do anything with this chapter desired.

In brief, the struggle toward our *total* reality ... this *hubris* which celebrates human potential, even at the cost of one's most cherished beliefs ... I call *"the Spirit of God."*

I have been an atheist in the worst possible sense these past few years ... by that I mean, I was merely a cultural *reaction*. I can now believe in something wonderful in existence — and I have learned that merely reacting, usually vehemently *against* or smugly *for* "God," ruins that wonderful sensation.

I cannot believe in a God which counts the hairs of *my* head, a God which is concerned with me in a personal way. However, I do believe in a general tendency in nature, this being something like "providence." I am often cared for though I toil not, nor spin. I would be willing to call the sensation which accompanies this acknowledgment, "God" — except that too many people, on either side of the issue, would take that statement and run too far with it. Lately I have been naming every cause of the wonderful sensation, "God" — taking care to become neither false nor smug, nor to use "God" as an "escape" from my reality.

If "God" represents the "indifferent" and "impersonal" in the mechanical universe, then must I use terms of neutral gender, "It" ...? Yet, I am not proposing a "pure pantheist's" definition by saying that "God is nature." I am saying that *the Kingdom of God is within me.* "God" represents a *particular* reflection of *my* reality — an orientation that only I can see. Then, being male myself, this God remaining inseparable from *my* identity, I had best refer to this "spirit" as male in gender. It then makes sense for a woman's God to take on the female gender — a Mother in Heaven — "She." What? Even Child-Gods for children? What delightfully mischievous scripture we would then have! No doubt, the two she bears would spin around and devour that bald-headed prophet for taking himself too seriously. (II Kings 2:23-24)

Do I love God so much that I would give up my immortality and the world Beyond in order to embrace Him in His manifested form? Do I love God's gift, my here and now?

Or do I reject the gift because I want something more ... something else?

It is divinely ironic that first we must renounce all claim to a Beyond and a personal Immortality before our love of God becomes genuine ... that is to say, *before we truly embrace this life.*

527

I do not know enough about Heaven to speak of eternal consequences. But in life itself — the one that ends after a few years — I have found only one sin possible: laziness ... to be inconvenienced by my own reality.

528

A unified religion in the world will be achieved, not through negotiation or social assimilation, but through enough individuals discovering and obeying repetition in Nature: *the cultivation of dignity ... the worship of the means to this end ... assigning such significance to the word "God."*

529

I thought I had fallen out with God, when in reality I had only found a better word to describe Him.

530

The goal of the atheist should be to put himself in a position where he no longer has the need to resist believers — and until that time comes, he *must* resist. Some lucky day in the future, an entire generation will no longer squander its time and energy in the God-AntiGod quagmire. And human progress will never before have seen anything like it — not that human progress is a substitute for God, but that the old name, "*God,*" had supplanted our drive toward real, physical progress.

531

Thus far "God" has been the word to explain *away* the world. What would happen if "God" became the word to explain our most elevated aspect upon *this world*?

532

The Holy Choice: The name "God" can serve the motives of humanity, as an eye patch to the horrible in reality ... or as the eye itself, naked, accepting every aspect on reality ... that unseen point from which we see our human existence.

533

Why are we more concerned with the name "God" than with the reality from which that name springs? If a man were to speak solely from within the framework of reality, he is "Godless." If a man were to speak solely from within the framework of a God of *another world*, then he is deluded. What if "God" became a word for the quest for significance in reality? Would we have missed the mark? From the believer's point of view we have begun with visible creation in order to understand a creator. From the realist's point of view we have begun with visible reality in order to pick up a challenge, the quest for significance, that is, to have a purpose ... a promise of fulfillment. Though the realist dare not call this quest "God," does it really matter if he does? Would he have something to offer the True Believer — improved leadership maybe — simply by his using the word, "God"?

534

Some will say, "*This* is not God." I say, "Agreed, but *that* is not God either." What *this* is I am still exploring, and this *exploring* fills me. Who cares for the name?

535

Why is *"Do I believe in God?"* not synonymous with *"Do I know how to live?"*

536

God is not in the sacrifice but in my increase. And where there is no sensation of increase there is no God.

537

How desperately we humans want to be complex ... delight in our inability to see around the last fact when the shadow of that last fact is nothing other than our own vanity. Anthropomorphism accounts for *all* of our confidence in the beyond, whether in religion, in metaphysics, or in a realist's "philosophy."

I propose that we begin to worship this anthropomorphism *for what it is*. Why not? We will never get around it, and it accounts for the universal prayer of the species: "Something *of me* in this too. Dear God!" An unrelenting effort to expose the anthropomorphic in every *leap away from our condition* would create a suffering ... a passion unequaled by all religious attempts thus far: this effort *not to leap* would be equally impossible but would have "authenticity" and tragedy on its side. What would become of this noble stage without this backdrop of *loss?* Without the futility of that loss? Why discard this one chance for the redemption of that futility? — not only to stare down this contradiction, but to fight to remain above it ... to the last.

538

More significant than the fact that there never was a theistic God is our *inability* to get beyond the "loss." We lament the shipwreck, when we should congratulate ourselves on the discovery of a new land.

539

It was not merely Christianity that had collapsed, but *everything* — except our neglected nature and the task to harness that nature toward another, higher task. We may console our loss of religion with this new task: it serves as a last obligation to ourselves.

540

What do we insects do with a word like "Hallowed?" Even in the distance it glows before us like a beacon. "We will fly after it!" ... and why not? Our materialism has no direction nor goal of its own. It stands before us in irrefutable silence, while we have at last found a light to fly after. Yet this *flying after* also belongs to our species, is material, and as such, is also irrefutable.

541

My reality invoking the highest sensations I call "God." In such a fullness how could I ever be so ungrateful as to ask for something *in addition*?

542

There is no difference between God and His Gifts. To have the one is to have the other.

543

I want a God in whom it is not demanded that I *believe* ... just as I want an existence where it is not demanded that I give up my senses or forget my condition in order to *get by*. Therefore, I equate the presence of God with the presence of mind, that is, the awareness of my condition ... without an appeal to a beyond. Who can deny the glory of immediate reality *within an ascending repetition?* The sensation is equal to gazing up into the heavens on a starlit night: the magnificence is not so much in the wonder as it is in the realization that such power is *real.*

544

The secret to any rebirth of spirit: to see the entire world as machine, man as nothing less — and *that-something-more* as that which is least tenable, most essential, the object of all our efforts, and no less than the spirit of God. Vanity is as light as air ... the human spirit is as a vapor ... as fuel is vapor ... and existence can ignite with the slightest friction against the commonplace.

545

The Truth is not the choice between "Material Reality" and "God" — nor the reconciliation between the two: this would presuppose them to be naturally separate and implacable enemies. The Truth not only shows how *Reality is God* but also reveals the process toward this realization ... the process whereby we become worthy of our own reverence.

546

The happiest things in life come of their own free will *after* I have labored and suffered vainly for their acquisition. This *providence* is that web of habits that support me above the mundane or dangerous ... that provide sweet fruits and increase health and understanding with sudden shocks of pleasure. *God*, however, is not that providence but the *trust* I place in that providence, the letting go of my cares and worries and knowing that through this repetition I am provided for ... *somehow.*

Still, there is that unavoidable moment, when we are forced to bear our cross, our realization, that God has, in the end, forsaken

170

us ... *after* we have been nailed to that horrible juncture. Godless, there is only *I* but this *I* thereupon is completed. An angel has arrived and rolled away the stone: *I*, as redeemer and son, have emerged in my Father's likeness — there is no God because I have *become* that God. Facing but defying the godless in the universe, I rise to an equal stature ... equal depth ... equal hardness to that of the cruelest fate. This too is providence.

547

The God Equation: I will not stand and stare at that chalkboard for too long. I want to thrust myself forward, not to linger or thrash about in the turbulence of argument and equation. Mere argument offers *justification,* which is only a thrashing about to stay afloat. It does not care for the phenomenon of force. It cares little that even iron will float with enough velocity. As a swimmer who propels himself forward by the movement of his own limbs, *by pushing away,* so do I push away each new argument and justification. An argument supports me *only as it propels me ... only as I leave it behind.*

Only in this manner can I skim the surface with ease and move in my chosen direction. I do not want to tread, thinking I have actually defined and justified myself, calculating that I have thereby fixed myself to the globe, while the current of the sea sends me five hundred miles south.

548

If there is an aspect upon reality that eludes definition, for which no one name seems to work better than another, why can I not call this "God?" Never mind that my word, "God," is not a "God" beyond this reality. I have to put this ineffable aspect somewhere, and I have this empty space within my breast ... in precisely that spot where I had already grown accustomed to reverence and worship. Overcoming my resentments with regard to failed religious attempts and although I have grown suspicious toward just this sort of pleasant sensation, I can find no objection. I can never be completely human as long as I deny myself the sensation of being more than human. "Not real," another says. Then is the "exclusion" of an obviously present sensation *real*? ... Possible? Can I say, "This sensation is mere vanity. From a strictly objective viewpoint upon the material world, this sensation is only the response of a stimulus. It has no existence outside of my private experience. It is no different from a cog spinning in a machine." ... and by saying this, do I end the reality of that sensation? Can I deny a part of reality without denying the whole of reality? Ought I to ascribe more reality to the emptiness than to the fullness? More to the "illegitimacy" of a sensation than to its existence?

There is no harm in speaking of God, just so long as one knows who He really is. The true God is sensation. He has always been sensation. Why does this revelation presuppose that I will now forsake Him? I would sooner forsake myself, knowing that He is the manifold sensation ... the illusion of my higher self. He is my desire to *make* this illusion a reality, not through denial of reality but through careful negotiations with that reality. God is found in this human sensation of *becoming*, whether I lack meaningfulness and am therefore searching it out, or whether I have it, for now, and am therefore sated with the fullness of being. God is chaos looking for order; God is also that exact moment of perfect order before that order explodes again into chaos. In opposition or confirmation, God is the demon of clarity I chase with this very passage.

Honor God by Opposing Him

549

I would rather keep my purity as an atheist than profane God by denying His creation. Thus, I claim there is no God with greater honesty than any believer, and I thereby deserve Him all the more.

550

This is Purity of Heart: to ask for nothing in return from God — not even that He exist. In fact, a saint could renounce all of the "world beyond" just so that his worship might become genuine.

551

An honest atheist is worth more than a smug "believer" — easy argument since there is no such thing as even an *honest* believer. Were I so wise and brave I would not even be the atheist ... since this is not a God-AntiGod world.

552

A genuine worship does not *make room* for God. On the contrary, it is just this *making room for God* which I attack, so as to elevate myself ... to feel that joy and dignity in the struggle toward honest conclusions.

553

To question toward is to pray. To act toward is to pray. To fail is to pray. But to accept facts beyond one's own experience ... to be a "genuine" follower ... to pay tithe for one's inherited obligations to the institution of averaged minds ... what is that?

What am I saying? That only the man who *challenges* God approaches the true God. He is a worthy *opponent*. Because he opposes, he is worthy of his own existence ... *worthy, because he has become its equal.* In this worthiness, what does he feel? What *sensation*? ... it is this new struggle toward reality — toward Truth — which I now feel as *the holy embrace of God.*

554

God is natural force in the universe, and spirituality is the human response to the inexorability of that force.

Is there comfort in knowing that our consciousness ... our identities are pieces separated from a whole? ... and that we will one day have as our "home-coming" a death which is cause for celebration? The redemption for our complete extermination being the return to that whole? The argument stands, but it waits out life as we grow thin and pale.

Or is there an even greater comfort in knowing that we are pieces of a whole but that we might, in this life, mock that whole in a sprightly dance *for this life* ... that we might mirror the glory of the universe in a brilliant and defying self-appropriation. Death arrives and there is cause for celebration here too ... but not necessarily for our return, but for our being equal to the very end.

If there is no God, then how can I oppose his non-existence? I am to take a stand, it seems, upon what is not there and so fall comically.

If there is no God, then "God" was only a word ... a representation of something *Human.* What is that *something*?

Hope of compensation? Is *this* life so horrible? And when it is indeed horrible, does *this* life have no compensation for those horrors?

Hope of Heaven? Is Hope a business contract where I am to forgo the luxury in this world so that I might have more luxury in the next?

Immortality? Is this another clause in the business contract, where I am to serve my master faithfully *only if* I am guaranteed an Eternal Pension? If I received no such guarantee, would I forsake my God? Is Hope cowardice? Does the word "God" represent nothing more than a *Human* fear of mortality?

If God is not the other-worldly, then perhaps God is that which persists in the *absence* of the above mentioned *vices.* The other-worldly is *not* irrelevant. Indeed, it is its *relevancy* that constitutes the problem — in precisely the same way in which any *foe* is relevant. *Other-worldliness opposes my sincerity. It is the great enemy to my love of this world.*

Perhaps the word "God" ... *"spirit of God"* represents that human pride which never gives Fate the satisfaction of seeing us knuckle under ... never reveals so much as any expression or gesture but that of defiance. I *rise up,* as the Greek tragic hero, in opposition, and precisely when and where I have every reason to fear and tremble I hold festivals to the joys and sufferings of *life!*

Conclusion: The Monument to Everlasting Joy

557

I have often suspected and it is only now beginning to prove itself true ... that I am not that "objective" creature I thought I was, but a puppy. I look around the trunk of the tree and eagerly chase that furry, happy tail until my indifferent master whistles me home again. I fly toward Him, happier than before, for I have no memory, not a very useful one anyway. Here we are again. I am the puppy. He is my master. And somehow I am uncontrollably happy with the situation.

558

What remains cheerful about *this life* and all of its particulars is that the "higher life" ... the "universal" is wholly dependent upon it. It is of *this life* and of all of its particulars from which the brain organizes itself into a *divine perception* of this life.

559

Where hope and reality meet there is joy. If one begins with hope and curtails reality, one's chances are slim. If one begins with reality and curtails hope, one stands a better chance.

560

The universe is not a riddle; it is man as riddle-maker who now stands disappointed before his own fact.

That we need riddles again but can no longer *believe* in them ... that we step outside of ourselves and helplessly watch hard facts grind our significance into pieces is unworthy of a species with a reflex for laughter.

561

To *participate* in everlasting joy, one must create and finish an independent work every day, such that it also serves as a brick to the great and final monument.

562

Beauty, joy, and strength are proofs.

563

Inevitably, the emphasis of a relationship moves from sex toward conversation. Whether one calls this change "evolution" or "devolution" reveals two important things about one's future: whether or not one is capable of finding a "spiritual" aspect upon one's reality and also, as a corollary, whether or not one is capable of even the smallest degree of happiness. And conversation just so happens to be one of the most *spiritual* of the types of happiness. An added blessing, and not at all obvious, is the very real *abundance* of this Joy: what is lost in immediate force is more than compensated by the nearly effortless, lifetime accumulation of little nothings into a consciousness rivaling the universe.

564

If one is strong enough, one's whole life can serve as preparation for today. A repeated action which is both "preparation" and "immediate satisfaction" is also called, "Joy."

565

A proposed repetition, when it succeeds in *affirming* my reality, has also succeeded in tethering my illusions to my reality.

Nothingness does not approach the horror of somethingness. Nothingness is a Lethe ... an escape ... room for something-like-the-God-of-Escape. With somethingness there is no door nor vent. One chokes on the air. The folly of the whole matter is that either aspect — *held to the exclusion of the other* — is an error. To have the one in the foreground is to force the other into the background. Life could be a meadow with flowers and children, and still we would only be capable of joy when the *entire question of something-nothing* were sent to the background by our preference for *these* joyful stimuli.

I would understand this foreign reality but that I no longer trust my interpreter. I have decided to stop listening to the translation and to observe directly the gestures and expressions as they manifest themselves. It is something like the expression of an exotic dance: I can take pleasure in it, but I have no adequate explanation for that expression ... no opportunity to sit back and meditate, for that damned interpreter keeps butting in and babbling on and on with his nonsense of *"that something more from this something less"* ... with his damned leaps: "Eternity! Infinity!" I am all too painfully aware of the explanation, that it never equals the beauty of the dance itself. Experience cloys with the slightest explanation. There is always something *too much*, and I begin to suspect that this something *too much* is nothing other than the addition of *Eternity*. It has been a very slow process, but I am finally getting my interpreter to acknowledge the disparity between *what he says* and *what I see*, and so now he is making statements like, "Man is limited. Man wants more. This is beautiful." But then I catch myself listening again. I have a right mind to stand up one of these times, let this interpreter ... this ... this *chaperone* stand back aghast; I would woo this twirling dancer, and the beauty would be in the awkwardness of that first kiss.

I am sure and confident, until I open my mouth to speak. This is the squeeze of our condition. We must speak to express our deepest feeling, but the act of this expression requires the compromise of individual feelings into universally accepted symbols. We are too big for the box of grammar and lose our tails when the box closes itself into a sentence. "But humans have no tails!" is the objection. We remain silent, for with the loss of our tails we have also lost our proof, and every attempt *to prove* incites laughter.

We *must* speak, but speaking is incomplete. We *feel* our meaning, but *speak* in absurdities. We are vessels that must pour out *this something within* but find no vessel without.

Perhaps what would satisfy us most would be a silent communication, one which required less of the pouring out of "mind" or "reflection" and more of the gratification of *a total experience*: for example, the sudden realization of potential ... or the exhibition of strength and beauty — an ecstatic pouring out *and receiving*, at the same time ... not really understanding this joy here and now ... *yet having it!* We identify our basic need for exaltation, as opposed to what we merely *want*. Once in this exalted state, we do not *satisfy* the "need" for communication, *but have eliminated that need altogether*. Joy is *the superfluity* that inevitably follows. It knows nothing of *"need"* or *"want."* It is enough to spill over. If there are no vessels to receive and contain ... well, what is that to *Joy*?

The brain is an organ capable of believing that there is no limit to the suffering it must pay for a limited gain ... and incapable, at the critical moment, of believing the opposite, that there is a limit to joy, until that opposite belief is not only unnecessary, but dangerously intoxicating. We teeter between misery and folly, but what would happen if we inched our way down the lever and stood, motionless, at the fulcrum point?

The social mind swings far and wide, like a pendulum, reaching out toward one illusion and then falling back with fear or disgust ... only to race out again toward another illusion.

But there is a narrower, faster *swing* available to the human experience ... and it is not the "middle ground" of opposing "causes" or "moralities" ... but the *coexistence* of two imaginary universes ... an overcoming of both *stark reality* and *wonder* over and over again ... training and practicing the reflexes ... perfecting one's observation skills so that the corrections become shorter and faster ... as one who tightens an iron string and takes joy in the vibration as it increases in pitch.

571

The "Good Life" is not the destination but the road, and a very narrow and winding road at that. Always just ahead we find a sharp turn toward a need so petty that we refuse to slow down for it. And where were we going anyway? The question itself leads us astray. As we admitted before, this is merely *a road*. But if we resign ourselves to a road without a known destination, what *striving toward* will keep us on *this* road? ... or at least allow us to cross it as many times as possible? ... for we cross the road so rarely and haphazardly that it seems inconsequential to the journey. But now I am getting ahead of myself again. Slower, slower ... not faster.